WHERE I'M FROM

Growing up Hip Hop...

By Ron Lawrence with Sheldon Taylor

Where I'm From: Growing Up Hip Hop

Copyright @ 2019 by Ron Lawrence

All rights reserved. No part of this book may be reproduced or transmitted in any form or by any means, electronic or mechanical, including photocopying, recording, or by any information storage and retrieval system, without the written permission of the Publisher, except where written by law.

Book design by Ron Lawrence

ISBN-13: 978-0-578-51228-

Printed in the United States of America

If you want to learn to swim, jump into the water. On dry land, no frame of mind is ever going to help you.

---Bruce Lee

CONTENTS

INTRO: These Three Words   11

Side I: Genesis (1914-1979)

Track One: The Hurst: The Black Gold Coast   17

Track Two: From Dominica to Queens   23

Track Three: Growing Up in The Hurst   37

Track Four: Music's Taking Over   53

Track Five: No Idea's Original   63

Track Six: Booty Land and Beyond   67

Track Seven: Uptown Baby   75

Side II: My Mic Sounds Nice (1979-1993)

Track Eight: My Turn   83

Track Nine: Step into A World of Ronnie Tuff   95

Chapter Ten: Idol Maker   113

Track Eleven: Howard, Hip Hop & Herby   123

Track Twelve: Puff   143

Track Thirteen: Two Kings in A Cipher   149

Side III: Movin' On 'Em (1993-2003)

Track Fourteen: Still Paying Dues	167
Track Fifteen: Mistaken Identity	171
Track Sixteen: Grinding in Cali	175
Track Seventeen: Everything I'm Hustling	181
Track Eighteen: Bad Boy	189
Track Nineteen: Makin' Moves with Puff	199
Track Twenty: Trinidad	205
Track Twenty-One: The King of New York	217
Track Twenty-Two: Scrambling	223
Track Twenty-Three: Life After Death	233
Track Twenty-Four: The Magic DAT	241
Track Twenty-Five: Flying High	255
Track Twenty-Six: Money, Power & Respect	275
Track Twenty-Seven: The Song That Almost Never Was	279
Track Twenty-Eight: Top of My Game	285

Side IV: Survivor
(2003-Infinity)

Track Twenty-Nine: Boombap and Bamboozled	299
Track Thirty: Luther	309
Track Thirty-One: Changes	315
Track Thirty-Two: Lights, Camera, Action	325
Track Thirty-Three: Strictly Business	329
Track Thirty-Four: Cipher Complete	337
Track Thirty-Five: Standing Strong & Staying Afloat	341
OUTRO: Can't Stop, Won't Stop	349

DIVINES

Cleve-o (The Turnout Brothers)	352
Salt	355
Hurby Luv Bug	356
Tone Fresh (Two Kings in A Cipher DJ)	358
D-Dot	361
Puffy	364
Younglord (Hitmen)	365
Brook Richardson (songwriter)	366
Tyrese	368
Benny Medina (music exec)	369

Where I'm From: Growing Up Hip Hop

To my sons Val Jr and Deston Ausar, this book is dedicated to both of you. When I started writing my life's story, I didn't realize how much I remembered about my history. Through memories going backward in time, I was able to observe the same characteristics in me that I see in each of you. Imagine if my parents recorded their biographies, there would be so much more I could tell you about them. It is for this reason I chose to document my life's experience. Now my story can live on endlessly in your hearts.

Where I'm From: Growing Up Hip Hop

Intro: These Three Words

I was eight years old. I was at summer camp on a hot day with my friends, headed for the pool. When we got there, I watched them jump in. I never learned how to swim but it didn't stop me from thinking that I could do it too. Now it's *my* turn to hit the water. My confidence quickly sunk when I realized that there was nothing underneath to hold me up. I was submerged in water from all sides. It felt like I was set adrift in a vast ocean with no land in sight. Frantically, I splashed around for what seemed like an eternity. The other kids in the pool finally figured out I couldn't swim. They got the lifeguard's attention. He pulled me out of the water and sends us home. I was crushed because I've ruined everyone's day.

I am from a beautiful country surrounded by water. I *live* in a community surrounded by water. Somehow, I never got around to learning how to swim. That pool experience traumatized me for years and I constantly had nightmares. Years later, my good friend Bret Lowery invites me to his wedding. When he introduces me to his mother, our eyes meet, and she recognizes me instantly. *"Oh my God,...you're the one that nearly drowned in the pool!"* Now I recognized her. Brett's mother was the lead summer camp counselor back then. Her voice beckoned dormant memories that I had long banished to the corners of my mind. I felt the heavy weight of every challenge and every obstacle---the numbing frustration of taking two steps forward, only to take three steps back. I remembered the turbulent oceans of adversity and failure that always threatened to take me under and three familiar words that always saved me: *gotta stay afloat*. Over the years, I would lean on these words for support and strength and no matter what happened, I always landed on my feet.

One of my favorite films of all time is Bruce Lee's *Game of Death*. Certain scenes keep me at the edge of my seat every time I see it, especially the ones with Bruce skillfully navigating a multi-level pagoda guarded by deadly adversaries on every floor. The same manner that Bruce used various martial arts fighting styles is the way I executed intense focus, concentration and hustle. Bruce defeated his opponents. I emerged victorious over the obstacles and struggles threatening to take me out.

These experiences would serve me well when I fought my biggest battle in 2016. *"Ronald, are you up yet? I will be there in 20 minutes."* My mother-in-law, Annette Douglas, called me to let me know she was on her way to take me to my doctor's appointment. I

Where I'm From: Growing Up Hip Hop

had just turned fifty a few months before and it was time for a colonoscopy. The doctor's office was only minutes away, so we arrived with time to spare.

I watched the nurse put an IV in my arm as I was being prepped for my procedure. Her voice was cheery and reassuring. *"Mr. Lawrence, this will take 20 minutes."* She was right. The procedure was quick. It seemed like I just closed my eyes. Now, I felt the weight of the doctor's hand on my shoulder easing me from my anesthesia-induced slumber. When he spoke, his words cut through my mental fogginess with the sharpness of a knife. *"You have cancer... I found cancer cells."* I struggled to grasp his diagnosis. All I could say was, *"for real?"* It was hard to conceive that I had cancer. I was extremely healthy. I didn't smoke or drink. I ate well. As I waited for my mother-in-law, I repeated the doctor's words in my head, trying to process what he just told me. When I told Annette the news, her reaction was the same. She was in disbelief. I was quiet for the rest of the ride home, thinking about what lay in store for me.

I had come a long way. Thirty-five years ago, I had embarked on hip-hop's long and winding road. I had seen and done it all. I was there as the park jams gave birth to a new kind of musical expression. Like a parent in awe of a baby's first steps, hip-hop slow but steady evolution excited me. Soon I went from spectator to participant. I wasn't an overnight success. I made it the hard way and like an Egyptian pyramid, I built my career brick by brick. *One beat and one rhyme at a time.* I hacked my way through the wilderness of the music business and made it to the mountaintop. I became a respected and highly successful music producer. Now here I was again, dropped into treacherous waters of uncertainty. I was in for the fight of my life and I would need to summon all the strength I had to stay afloat.

Where I'm From: Growing Up Hip Hop

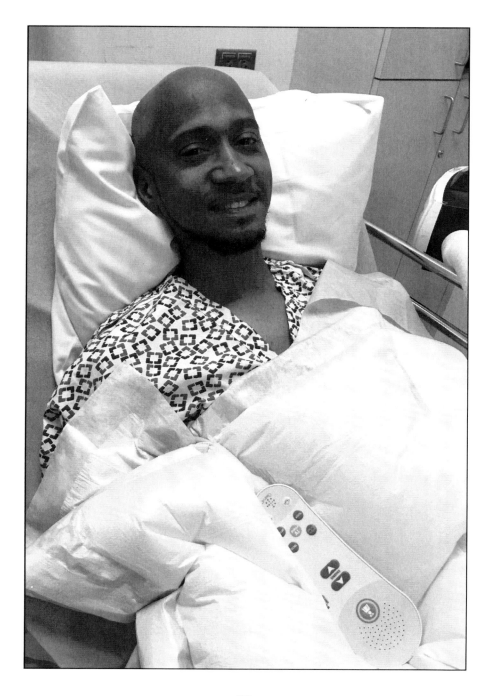

SIDE I

Genesis (1915-1978)

Where I'm From: Growing Up Hip Hop

Track One
<u>The Hurst: The Black Gold Coast</u>

Everything I have ever done and continues to do go back to the place where I'm from. You may know it as East Elmhurst, but we call it *The Hurst*. It borders the neighborhood of Corona in the northwest section of Queens, just minutes away from LaGuardia Airport. East Elmhurst is a solidly middle-class area with attached Cape Cods and multi-family homes. Beneath my neighborhood's modest make-up is a rich history virtually unknown to anyone outside of New York City.

Back in the forties and fifties, East Elmhurst was known as New York City's Black Gold Coast. Long before black New Yorkers lived in downtown penthouses and upstate mansions, East Elmhurst and Corona were *the* destinations for affluent Harlemites. Rigid housing restrictions and racist covenant agreements kept them out of certain areas.

Queens had become an attractive option but "gateway" neighborhoods near Manhattan like Sunnyside were out. So were Jackson Heights and Forest Hills. East Elmhurst and Corona were

Where I'm From: Growing Up Hip Hop

more accommodating. Louis Armstrong was the first of the black elite to move out to the area. While he was away on tour, his wife bought a place on 107th Street. Instead of moving out to Jersey, Connecticut or Westchester, he stayed put and lived in Corona for the rest of his life. Dizzy Gillespie moved around the corner to 106th Street and soon after that other jazz guys like Clark Terry, Cannonball Adderley and his brother Nat (his son Nat, Jr worked with Luther Vandross later) and Jimmy Heath would follow.

Ella Fitzgerald and her husband, bassist Ray Brown, lived in the larger homes on Ditmars Boulevard that overlooked Flushing Bay and LaGuardia Airport. Reverend William Gardner also lived on Ditmars. He was an early mentor of a young Martin Luther King who had preached some of his first sermons at First Baptist Church on Astoria Boulevard.

Prominent athletes lived in East Elmhurst like Willie Mays and Tommie Agee from the Mets. Ray Felix from the Knicks also lived in the neighborhood. So did Bobby Hammond from the Giants. When he was getting in shape for games, he worked out at 127 Park. Bill Kenney from the Inks Spots lived in the area for a while. Harry Belafonte had a home on 25th Avenue. Malcolm X had a place on 97th Street a few houses from where I lived.

The working-class people living in Harlem and other surrounding areas also wanted a chance to grab a piece of the American Dream. A place with a yard or maybe even a garage.

Where I'm From: Growing Up Hip Hop

Teachers, postal workers and bus drivers saved their money and bought homes in East Elmhurst. Caribbean families gravitated to the area as well. Some like my father worked at the airport. Others worked at hospitals. Some had city jobs. A real estate agent from Barbados relocated to The Hurst from the Bronx. His son Eric Holder--would later become a judge and a future US attorney general.

As more blacks moved to East Elmhurst, whites moved to Long Island and other sections in Queens. Harry Belafonte's autobiography *My Song: A Memoir of Race, Art, and Defiance* tells a revealing story of how white flight provided his young daughter her first taste of racism. She came home one day and told him that their family would have to move because her white "friends" told her "niggeroos" (Negroes) were living in the neighborhood.

When discriminatory housing practices loosened up for black people, Belafonte bounced to Central Park West and Dizzy Gillespie headed out to Jersey (I'd do the same later). While some left the Hurst for greener pastures, others stayed put. The stability of the neighborhood ensured we would not be affected by white flight, a declining tax base and loss of industry sector jobs that devastated black communities in the 1960s and 1970s. Because everybody shopped in the neighborhood, all the money stayed in the community. The Nation of Islam had a strong presence here. I remember they had a bakery, a record shop, and a seamstress in the neighborhood.

Where I'm From: Growing Up Hip Hop

During the 1976 Blackout, we didn't experience the major riots and looting that took out main shopping drags in other cities. On Astoria Boulevard, things were quiet. I don't remember anything jumping off except for maybe a small burglary at a bike shop on Northern Boulevard. One of the worst things that ever happened in my neighborhood was a bombing on 96th street. A member of the Armed Forces for Federal Liberation (FALN) accidentally set off a pipe bomb he was making. I remember the police cars and fire trucks surrounding the block and the incident being on the local news. Another time during the Christmas holidays, a mother and her boyfriend killed her two children and burned them up afterwards.

People remained in the neighborhood for decades. Our diversity was our strength. We had Muslims and Christians. Black preachers and Black Panthers. Athletes and entertainers. Professionals and working-class people. They represented a *true* example of a New York melting pot. Today, East Elmhurst survives and thrives. It is more diverse these days, but it still holds its own in terms of equity and value. Gentrified up-and-coming neighborhoods may come and go, but the Hurst will never lose its appeal. It symbolized a time when Black celebrity revolved around its own orbit.

How many places can you say that had working-class people living near their upper-middle-class celebrity neighbors? How many musicians today can say that when they came from off tour, they would be welcomed back home by the entire neighborhood? How many kids can say they could walk up to Malcolm X and have a conversation or chill on the stoop with Louis Armstrong shooting the breeze, enjoying Good Humors on a hot summer day? There is an old-school term that we used back in the day: *around the way*. It conjures up images of home-town pride. A celebration of the communal neighborhood spirit that inspired a different kind of celebrity---not the kind holed up in the mansions of Beverly Hills and Bel-Air. I'm talking about the kind of black star power you could see, touch and feel. A galaxy of hip-hop stars like no other.

You could live around the way and still drive a Rolls or a Benz. One rapper had six cars in the driveway. People thought he was a drug dealer, but he was just a regular guy content with living with his grandmother instead of chilling in a condo secluded in a high-brow neighborhood (which eventually, he did). Our hometown spirit and creative energy was not just in the Hurst. It was over in Astoria, Hollis and South Jamaica. It existed in "Strong Island," out in areas like Wyandanch, Brentwood, Roosevelt and Hempstead.

When we shouted out our neighborhoods in liner notes, on wax and live onstage, we made New York City seem like one of the seven wonders of the world. We inspired people all over the world who loved hip-hop to look inside themselves and produce their own version of what we were doing in New York City.

Where I'm From: Growing Up Hip Hop

97 St in East Elmhurst, Queens. The home I grew up in

Where I'm From: Growing Up Hip Hop

Track Two
<u>From Dominica to Queens</u>

My story begins in Dominica, my native country where I was born on November 14, 1965. Dominica is a country in the West Indies that was a British colony for years. It has a history of being a progressive place. Fifty years before blacks in America held public office, Dominica was the first Caribbean country that was completely self-governed by black people. Dominica also elected the first female prime minister who would serve three terms---the longest in the country's history.

    My great-aunt Irene blazed the trail to America first. She left Dominica on an ocean liner, passing through Great Britain before arriving in Harlem in 1915. There were no airports in New York back then, so ocean liners were the mode of travel for immigrants coming to New York City.

    Back then, Harlem was a neighborhood in transition. The Jewish community was moving out and African-Americans and West Indians were moving in. When the Jewish property owners moved to the Bronx and Westchester, they rented out the vacant apartment buildings they left behind.

Uptown was America's spiritual and cultural Black Utopia but there was another side to Auntie Irene's Harlem as well. It was a pressure cooker filled with the ingredients of social inequity, a boiling cauldron reeking of frustration's bitter aroma. Displaced aggression and detached empathy were chained together in the hold of a vessel bound for collision with no course correction in sight. Harlem soared creatively and culturally, but in terms of economics, it barely left the ground.

Cramped apartments were subdivided to accommodate the influx of people pouring in from the South and the Caribbean, leading to mass overcrowding and inferior living conditions. Buildings left in the care of unscrupulous landlords fell into disrepair. Uninhabitable properties were set on fire. Their owners collected the insurance money and moved on.

White merchants owned many of the businesses in Harlem, sometimes charging the highest prices for the most inferior product, from groceries to furniture. Every shop on 125th Street from the mom and pop establishments to major stores refused to hire from a black labor pool who just happened to be their customers. The revenue the merchants earned never stayed in Harlem. They took it with them to build their own communities away from the people who patronized their businesses.

Where I'm From: Growing Up Hip Hop

Auntie Irene was an entrepreneur. She owned a beauty shop, so she was spared the indignity of being denied access to avenues of upward mobility offered to white ethnics but out of reach to many of her people. It was time for a change. And like so many others, she looked to Queens.

While Auntie Irene's zip code might have changed, that strong sense of self she cultivated back in Dominica had not. To paraphrase a line from Randall Robinson's book *Quitting America: The Departure of a Black Man from His Native Land,* the self-awareness of my homeland had sprung from a culture moving across time like a broad river collecting, forgiving and leaving behind nothing. West Indians were firmly interwoven within the tapestry of class, economics, and occupation.

We might have been under British rule, but we were left to our own devices compared to black Americans subjected to a system of oppression enforced by law and violence. As West Indians, our lives were different. This doesn't mean that racism was non-existent, our reality was just different. My father was steadily advancing in his law enforcement career and Dominica was pushing for complete control of its internal affairs when the Civil Rights Act was just being signed in America.

Our strong ties to family and country made us even stronger. We may have looked to America for a better life, but we did not require social validation or acceptance. Because of this, our nature and attitude characterized by independence were often misunderstood. West Indians were the target of ridicule, envy, and hatred. Our upward mobility reflected how far we had come and was a reminder to the outside world how far everyone else had to go. If you watch the last couple seasons of the TV series *Boardwalk Empire*, you will see examples of the uneasy dynamic that existed between West Indians and African-Americans.

Auntie Irene did not just leave Dominica and Harlem on her own quest for upward mobility. She also sponsored our move from Dominica to Queens. Her strength and generous spirit were like that of many Black women helping others coming up from the South or the Caribbean looking for work. They fed and housed them while helping them navigate new surroundings. They flipped their skills into professions that allowed them to maintain their dignity in the face of limited opportunities for women at the time. Others swallowed their pride to give their children a better life.

Some Black women stood on Harlem street corners like auction blocks in search of "day work" in neighborhoods they would never live in, scrubbing floors and working in the kitchens of white households. That history is captured in a song from my childhood---*I Will Always Love My Mama*. The song's lyrics were real for me. It reminds me of my Moms cooking and doing what she had to do to take care of us.

Where I'm From: Growing Up Hip Hop

Moms was a teacher back in Dominica but when she got to America, her credentials were not accepted so she was forced to go back to school get a GED. Here she was, a professional woman in her late thirties sitting in class with a bunch of high school dropouts she was supposed to be teaching! She also cleaned houses on the side to supplement our household income. I marvel at the strength my mother had to have been able to swallow her pride like that.

After she got her GED, Moms enrolled at Brooklyn College part-time and eventually got her master's degree in mathematics. On top of her work and her studies, Moms also found time to tutor the neighborhood kids on weekends for extra money. Moms' life revolved around work and school. She would leave home at 6:30 in the morning when she started working at Junior High School 117 in downtown Brooklyn, she kept right on going to school.

Her schedule was the same for years. She would walk in the house by 7:30 in the evening. While she graded papers, she worked on her studies at the same time. Sometimes I would catch her dozing off at the kitchen table. I can still see her now, coming down the block after a long day of work, with two grocery bags in each arm. Moms stayed busy.

Moms minored in music in college. She loved Mozart and could play classical piano very well. She also loved to sew. She was so good that she made all the clothes she wore for work. Her and Pops worked as a team. He held it down and cooked dinner. When she got home, he would head off to work.

Pops was a high-ranking law enforcement officer. Guns were banned from the island, but he kept things in line. He was strict and a stickler of discipline which made people fear and hate him in equal measures. Law enforcement was his life's passion. Pops was in his early forties when he moved to Queens and well past the mandatory age of becoming a New York City policeman. He ended up getting a job with American Airlines. He also did security part-time. During those early New York days, he did not drive. It did not matter though because LaGuardia was right down the street and he could walk to work.

My parents were both very practical when it came to their choice of occupations. Pop's job at American Airlines allowed family members to fly standby for free but there were strict regulations. We had to dress professionally. A shirt-and-tie type of thing. You kept to yourself and did not interact with the other passengers. This benefit eased the financial burden of the entire family traveling back to Dominica for vacations and holidays.

When we enrolled in school, Moms taught us for a while to make sure we had the fundamentals down. She even took it a step further with me. On weekends and during summer breaks, Moms had me in the books. I brushed up on my reading, writing and math skills.

Where I'm From: Growing Up Hip Hop

When I was done, she would make me drink a glass of milk afterwards (which I hated) before I could go outside to play.

It was hard. There were eight of us---my mother and father, four brothers, three sisters and me but Dad had a total of 12 children. He had three before he met my mom. We went from having a privileged life with servants and maids to living in an apartment until my parents were able to buy a two-family home. We lived on the bottom floor and rented out the top. As an adult, I look back at the sacrifices and challenges as they strived to make it America. It is why I will honor my great-aunt, grandmothers, my parents, and my immigrant story forever.

When we first came to Queens in the late sixties, I went back to Dominica while my parents set up shop. I was three or four years old. The two years I spent without them seemed like ten. I thought they were gone forever and would *never* come back for me. In the meantime, I kept myself occupied doing all kinds of crazy things I shouldn't have been doing. I was a daredevil back then. I'm not sure where it came from, but my fearless nature came early.

I can recall traveling to the countryside to see my grandmother and enjoying the ride up the steep mountain when I heard sounds of tires sliding against the gravel. Rocks were hitting the glass with the force of bullets. I looked out the window and I saw the car virtually sliding off the cliff. The back tires were literally hanging in the air.

Where I'm From: Growing Up Hip Hop

The driver quickly managed to regain control but after that experience, nothing scared me. Anything considered off-limits, I was going to try because I thought I could do it! I remember at five years old jumping on the back of a pickup truck. I lost my balance and skinned up my knees and elbows. The permanent scars left behind continue to remind me to watch out for dangerous situations.

I was happy to when they finally came and got me. Just as Auntie Irene brought her strong identity with her from Dominica, I took my sense of recklessness along with me to Queens.

When I got back to New York, there was no way anyone could keep me in the house. My father couldn't understand why I would always come home at inappropriate hours. He never made the connection that my rebellious streak came from the freedom I enjoyed back in Dominica. I would always find ways to sneak out. It was nothing for me to climb out of every window in our house. Once I got out, I was free to roam.

One winter, I went to 127 Park to meet my friends. We were playing chase when I fell headfirst through some broken wooden floorboards and landed on an iron beam. I must have fallen ten or twelve feet. I busted my chin open and the cut was so bad, you could see the white meat. I racked my brain trying to figure out how I was going to tell Pops. I ended up covering it up with a Band-Aid instead of having it looked at.

Where I'm From: Growing Up Hip Hop

It was a bad idea. I could have gotten an infection, but there was no way I was going to risk incurring Pop's wrath. I learned a huge lesson that day. I would learn a few more because most of the time I ended up getting caught. I got that ass spanked many times!

Once I invited myself on a friend's family trip to Coney Island. The trip was a two-hour ride from East Elmhurst. Back then I had a weak stomach and could not take long car rides. I threw up all over everyone in the backseat, ruining the trip for everybody.

I used to have a lot of nightmares. I would wake up the whole house in the middle of the night. In some of my dreams, I could see tiny people the size of my hand walking around living in their own city. Once, I remember seeing a little man on a horse. There was a huge tree outside my window and every night it turned into a monster right before my eyes.

Once my parents took me to a beach and I saw a small cruise ship with little people in it. Finally, they just couldn't take it anymore and took me to a priest. It was four in the morning. When we got there, he prayed over me. I'm not sure if it worked or I eventually grew out of it, but I never had nightmares or saw strange things anymore.

Where I'm From: Growing Up Hip Hop

Me at 5 months old and my sister Beverly (R.I.P.)

Where I'm From: Growing Up Hip Hop

Sylvester Desilva Lawrence (Dad)

Where I'm From: Growing Up Hip Hop

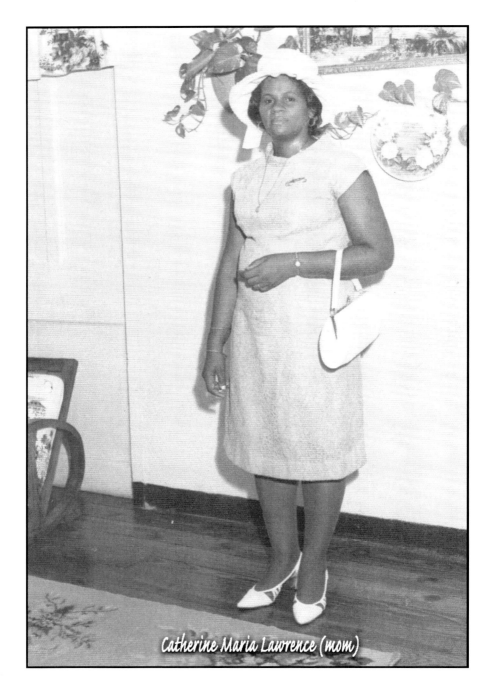

Catherine Maria Lawrence (mom)

Where I'm From: Growing Up Hip Hop

Where I'm From: Growing Up Hip Hop

Track Three
<u>Growing Up in The Hurst</u>

My first day of school was rough. Back in 1972, it was not easy being a West Indian kid with an accent. There were other kids in the neighborhood who were Caribbean, but they never let on. There was no way I could hide my accent, so they all knew. All the first graders would make fun of me.

My first fight was with a little boy named Ricky. He lived across the street from me. Ricky would bother me every day until one day he and I had a fist fight at the bus stop after school. While we were fighting, my bus stop tag that was pinned to my coat fell off. In the middle of the fight, Ricky picked it up and gave it to me. We became the best of friends after that.

I had to get up on the fashions. *Quick.* All the kids had Pro-Keds, a fly canvas sneaker with a thick rubber sole. You could always tell the real ones because they had a red and blue stripe at the toe. No matter how much you kept' em clean, once you couldn't see those stripes it was time for another pair! My mom bought me skips from Junction Boulevard. Skips were the cheapest sneakers you could find back then. They barely had any traction and once you run through them for a month, the soles would have holes in them. The kids let me have it so bad that every day I came home from school I *begged* my moms to buy me a pair of Pro-Keds. When she finally gave in and bought me a pair, I felt like the coolest kid ever!

I never owned a bike or had a lot of toys, but my mom made sure I had clothes on my back. That was cool because even at nine and ten years' old my fashion game had to be on point. I wanted to fit in, so I insisted she buys me the cool stuff. I would look around to see what the cool kids were wearing and have her buy me the same thing.

In the winter, I had to have a heavy blue snorkel coat with the oversize furry hood that made me look like an aardvark when I pulled it over my head. I had rubber soled earth shoes that were just as comfortable as a pair of sneakers. Instead of jeans, I wore bell bottom dress pants that draped over my sneakers just right. From there, I moved onto gabardine slacks from a store called AJ Lester's. We called them AJ's for short. I wore double knits with seams down the legs.

As I got older, styles were changing fast, so I had to keep up. When pleated pants came out, I jumped on those. A year after, that I was the wearing the ice cube design. Soon I left the Pro-Keds behind for Pumas and switched to bell bottoms Lee jeans when they became the style. My jeans had creases in them. I would use up a half a can of starch to make my creases look sharp. You could see the imprint of iron burn marks on my jeans. Sometimes I would have the local tailor from the cleaners sew them in. I took my appearance *very* seriously.

When it came to my sneakers, I was very meticulous. Having busted sneakers were a no-no. If you stepped on someone's foot, you had to be ready to fight. New York is a pedestrian town and a fresh pair of sneakers could take a beating. You had to always have your tools with you at all time to deal with scuffs and the dirt. If you had suede sneakers, they needed extra care. You couldn't wear 'em in the rain and they could get dirty pretty fast. You constantly had to brush them to keep up the knap. They always had to look fresh. My friends and I always kept a toothbrush in our back pockets. We would usually clean our sneakers in the park or on the street. It didn't matter where we were because at the first sign of unsightly debris, we went to work!

I was serious about my sneaker game. How serious? Listen--- I remember when the very first Air Jordans came out. I copped the red-and-black ones. They cost $100 which was a lotta money in '84. I walked into the store and told the guy *"let me get those."* Didn't even ask about the price. You know the old saying, *"if you have to ask...."*

I was feeling *good* when I brought those sneakers home. Before I put them in the closet, I opened the box one last time and pulled them out. The soles were gleaming. Pristine. The leather was so damn shiny, I could almost see my reflection. I handled those sneakers as if they were fine crystal. I held them up to the light as if I were examining the cut of an exquisite diamond. As I sat in the silence of my room, I could hear them call out to me, begging me to put them on. I suppressed the temptation. Even the dopest pair of sneakers looked wack if the rest of your gear was not on point. My urges would have to live to fight another day. I carefully put 'em back in the box as if I was placing baby Jesus in the manger.

It didn't take three wise men to find out what happened a few weeks later when it came time to break 'em out. I opened the Nike box and could not believe what I saw. My sneakers were busted. Disfigured. My sneakers were on life support and *nothing* could save them. They looked like Michael Jordan played all 82 games in them. *Outside.* My younger brother Lyburd snuck in my closet and wore them to school. He wore those sneakers *one day.* When I saw Lyburd, I lunged at him like Linc Hayes from the Mod Squad and damn near tried to kill him. To top it off, his feet were too damn big for the shoes. I made him pay me back. Years later, when Lyburd admitted to me that he would sneak and wear all my clothes, we had a good laugh about it.

Let's take a mental trip down memory lane. Close your eyes and take a walk with me up Astoria Boulevard as we head past McDonald's, the Fair movie theater, the Cozy Cabin and Burger King. The Buccaneer and Deerhead diners are packed with the afternoon crowds. Across 94th Street is Butts Realty, Freddie and

Nettie's and Pressley's drug store. We walk a little further. Now we're on 97th Street. Mr. Murphy's corner store is in sight. In the mornings, the aroma of their hot rolls, fresh out the oven always drew people from the neighborhood to his store.

We stop at the record shop. Harold Melvin and the Blue Notes' *Bad Luck* blasts from outdoor speakers on the sidewalk. The funky bassline draws us in like a Philly Soul pied piper. The smell of smoky incense and the eye-catching neon light posters are intoxicating. We decide to stay awhile.

We hit the racks, flipping through the latest releases while Teddy's frantic screams make him sound like a man on fire. As he calls on Jesus to save him, the heavens open to the sound of The Isley Brothers' *Who's That Lady*. Ernie Isley's blistering guitar and big brother Ronnie's vocals waft through the air like a summer breeze: The guy at the counter smiles as we dance to the music. Then he throws on The O'Jays. We recognize the congas instantly---*I Love Music!* Next up is James Brown—no wait---that's *Express* from BT Express. I heard they were from over in Brooklyn. Kool and the Gang brings us down from our high. *Summer Madness* is a welcome sonic rainbow after our soulful rain shower.

I had so many great experiences as a kid growing up in the Hurst. I ate cheeseburgers and Swedish Fish candy from Cunningham's. I went to Tony the barber for haircuts and attended Cub Scout meetings at First Baptist Church. In the summers I went to

Where I'm From: Growing Up Hip Hop

ABC camp on Northern Boulevard with a lot of my old crew. I also made a lot of new friends from all parts of the town.

Saturday mornings were cleanup time. All of us kids were expected to help Moms clean up. While my older sister vacuumed, my job was to polish the floor model TV in the living room. You know the kind. The heavy joints with the wood finish. I would shine it down so good that it looked like it was just purchased from the showroom floor. It had all the latest features like a big VHF/UHF antenna on top. There were knobs you could turn for better reception and channel surfing (there was no remote control, by the way). When you changed the channel, it was like trying to crack a safe combination. When it was time for Soul Train, we looked forward to seeing performances of our favorite artists that we heard on the radio. We loved groups like The Jackson Five, but we always hoped to see the artists who created the songs that were being played at neighborhood park jams around New York.

In my spare time, I liked to draw. I would buy Marvel Comics, just so I could draw Spider-Man. I also drew Woody Woodpecker or any character that was cool to me. In a large family, it can be easy to get lost in the shuffle. Younger siblings might be left to fend for themselves while the older ones go out in the world and do their own thing. I am happy to admit that this was not my life. I was able to witness everything my siblings were into within the confines of home. I always found something interesting to latch on to.

Where I'm From: Growing Up Hip Hop

Back in the 70s before computers and cellphones, it was all about *activity*---the pursuit of hobbies or whatever you were into. In my home, there was enough of that to go around. I had four brothers who had a variety of interests and they always included me in what they are doing. I became a curator of many styles and pulled from each one of them. Soon, I would carve out my own interests that would lead me down a road of curiosity, creativity and ambition for the rest of my life.

During every holiday or special event, my brother Earl always took pictures and videos with his 35millimeter camera, capturing everything that went on. His photos were always high quality and I still have them. Every time I look at them, I marvel at how great the images were and how skilled my brother was back then and at such a young age. Earl was also into making videos, taping everything that we did. The oldest of my mother's children, Earl was a student at Pace University. He was heavily into his Dominican culture and was proud of it. An avid collector of *Ebony*, *Jet* and *Right On* magazines, Earl was an archivist by heart. I would pick up that from him later.

Earl opened me up to a world outside my window. He was the one in the family who took us younger siblings on outings because my parents were always working. He took my sisters and me to Eastern Parkway for the annual West Indian carnival. We went to the Fair Theater on Astoria Boulevard to see blaxploitation flicks like

Where I'm From: Growing Up Hip Hop

Three the Hard Way. Earl took us everywhere from amusement parks to holiday parties at his job in Manhattan.

Derickson was into fashion and did his own photo shoots. He would let me tag along and take his pictures for him. During photo shoots in Flushing Meadows Park, Derickson would set up the camera and show me how to use the viewfinder to capture the image correctly. These experiences helped me develop my eye and fueled my future interest in photography and film production. Derickson was very smooth when it came to dealing with the ladies. He could also be strict and serious like my pops. He didn't like to play around. Derickson was so smart that he skipped one grade ahead and won a wrestling scholarship to Howard University at the age of 16. When he got to Howard, he pledged Omega Psi Phi. He would go into politics later.

Michael was the smartest one in the family. He inherited Moms' love of math and classical music. Mike was a self-taught pianist. He was a straight-A student in calculus and physics and skipped two grades to graduate when he was 15 years old. Since he and Derickson both graduated from high school in the same year, Mike wanted to follow him to Howard, but Moms thought he was too young to go away. He was also into martial arts and would teach me things. Being a huge Bruce Lee fan, I jumped in head first, studying the Eagle Claw style---a series of pressure point strikes and hand-to-hand grappling styles.

Where I'm From: Growing Up Hip Hop

When martial arts flicks like *Fist of Fury, Chinese Connection* and *Enter the Dragon* played at the Fair, I would envision myself on the screen. Pops worked security there, so we got in for free. The Fair was on 92nd and Astoria Boulevard and was named after the very first World's Fair that came to New York in 1939. It was five blocks from my house and was like my second home. The latest releases were only a dollar and fifty cents so sometimes I could catch double features, two for the price of one.

The very first martial arts film I ever saw was *Five Fingers of Death*. There were others like *Hong Kong Cat, Deadly China Doll,* and *Duel of the Iron Fist.* These movies were great, but the ones that really made a lasting impression on me were the Bruce Lee joints. When I first saw *Fist of Fury* and *Chinese Connection* back in 1973, I came out of the movie theater excited. I wanted to be just like Bruce. To say I idolized him would have been an understatement.

If you were a male growing up in the early 70's, Bruce was definitely an inspiration whether you were white or black. There is a scene in *Saturday Night Fever* where John Travolta's character is in the mirror getting ready to go out. The camera pans to a picture of Bruce with nunchucks in his hand and quickly cuts back to Travolta flexing in the mirror imitating Bruce. Everybody loved Bruce back then. My bedroom wall was filled with posters of my hero. Any magazine featuring Bruce that I could get my hands on**,** I grabbed it for my collection. I even had the Kung Fu slippers and outfit to match.

Where I'm From: Growing Up Hip Hop

New York was martial arts crazy. Karate schools started to pop up around the city, capitalizing on the Bruce Lee phenomenon. There was one on Junction Boulevard and another in Flushing, not far from my neighborhood. I walked for blocks just to visit the martial arts studios to read the magazines and look at the weapons. I began to hone my art skills by sketching Bruce Lee portraits I saw in magazines.

I spent countless hours every day perfecting my skills, modeling Bruce's impeccable focus and flair. He had a simple philosophy that I took to heart, applying it to everything I did: *Be like water*. Bruce's movements were flawless---quick and tight, flowing like water, I believe the creative process in making music should be the same way. When I began making beats years later, I strived to become a perfectionist. I also loved blaxploitation movies like *Black Belt Jones*, *The Soul of Nigger Charlie*, *Super Fly*, *Scream Blacula, Scream*, and *Cleopatra Jones*. I remember being eight years old and being mesmerized by cool guys like Fred Williamson, Jim Kelly and those guys on the screen. They were my heroes too.

A day at the Fair was like a scene right out of the film *Cooley High*. Smoked filled air. Chewing gum on the floor. People cheering during the action and fight scenes. Then there were the fights. All it took was someone from Corona to say something to set things off.

I had great relationships with my sisters too. I had three of them---Christobelle, Beverly and Bernie. They were very good looking. All the older guys on the block tried to be cool with me so that they could get next to my sisters. Of course, Pops was not having it and he would always run them away. Chrissy liked to draw, play the piano, sing and she loved to run track. After she graduated in 1980, she went to Howard too, continuing the family tradition. Beverly was rebellious like me. She loved to hang out at an early age and go to parties. I followed her, but I knew my limits. Bev got in trouble more often than I did. Bernie was the youngest. She was the tattletale. I would get in trouble a lot because Bernie would always rat me out. She had a lot of friends and they all were pretty. Just about all the girls that she brought to the home would end up liking me and I would have little flings with them. She also loved to sing. In fact, she was good enough to be accepted into Manhattan's High School of Music and Art where she met future rap stars Dana Dane and Slick Rick.

Bernie and I were very close because we were the youngest. Just like I tagged along with my brothers, Bernie followed me to a lot of places where I introduced her to the beat of the street that would become hip-hop. Because of the large age gap between my siblings, me and Bernie were usually paired up. I can still see my sisters now playing double Dutch in the street or us playing freeze tag. We would play red light, green light, 123 and skelly while songs like The Spinners' *Could It Be I'm Falling in Love* were on the radio. When it got dark and the lamppost lights came on, we would sit on the porch and tell stories or jokes.

Lyburd was the youngest of my father's children. He came to New York a little later. He was getting into trouble back in Dominica, so my parents sent for him. He always reminded me of myself when I was young---a kid with funny clothes and a funny accent, trying to fit in. My older brother Dony was the biggest and strongest in the family *and* around the neighborhood. He had huge muscles for a guy his age. You could not miss my brother with his huge, round Afro and thick West Indian accent that he has never shaken to this day. Dony was also a DJ. I had no idea that watching him in action would change my life forever.

Where I'm From: Growing Up Hip Hop

Where I'm From: Growing Up Hip Hop

Where I'm From: Growing Up Hip Hop

Where I'm From: Growing Up Hip Hop

Track Four
<u>Music's Taking Over</u>

It's Labor Day 1975. I am watching my brother Dony stand in front of two turntables in deep concentration. Huge headphones are on his head. The Ritchie Family's *Brazil* is whipping the crowd into a frenzy. Dony plucks a record from the crate behind him and places it on the turntable. He finds the right song and gives the record a few backspins. When he slides a lever over to the right, pandemonium breaks loose. As *Brazil* fades out, The Jackson Five's *Forever Came Today* sprang forward like daylight savings time and the crowd goes wild.

That was the day Earl drove Dony and me out to Eastern Parkway for a gig in Brooklyn. Dony was playing at the annual Caribbean Labor Day Carnival, an elaborate festival promoting West Indian pride with lots of parades along with the great food and Caribbean music we grew up on.

We also heard records by Jamaican and Afro-British funk bands like The Beginning of the End and Cymande. Their songs

Where I'm From: Growing Up Hip Hop

Funky Nassau, Come Down Baby and *Bra* were laced with strong rhythms and heavy percussion seamlessly blending in with traditional reggae and soca sounds. One record I loved to hear was Manu Dibango's *Soul Makossa*. It was, as we used to say---*the joint*. That record was everywhere. It rocked the festival and the clubs. It was on the radio and in the streets. We heard it in the park. It was a simple song. Just bass, drums and horns. Powerful. It was crazy how many lives that record had. Michael Jackson and Rihanna used it. Kool and the Gang's *Jungle Boogie* was inspired by it.

Every year, I looked forward to soaking up the energy at the festival but watching my brother spin was the definite highlight. Dony Dancemaster and his emcee Al (and later Night Train) were one of the many mobile DJ crews playing all over the city. He usually rolled with two or three friends who helped him to carry speakers and records to whatever park they would jam at. Dony had a Black 1976 Ford Econoline van he used to transport his equipment around to his DJ gigs.

As a young boy, I was front and center for the mobile DJ culture planting the seeds for what would become hip hop. For me it started with watching DJ crew Nu Sounds jam in 1973 and watching Dony play in 127 Park in the summer of 1975.

There were also King Charles and Disco Twins who were some of the main DJs from East Elmhurst. Their popularity inspired the formation of Queens DJ crews from Jamaica, Queensbridge and

Where I'm From: Growing Up Hip Hop

Astoria. Dony came out of the mobile DJ tradition that began with older guys like Flowers, Maboya, Pete DJ Jones and Plummer back in the late 60s and early 70s. Because of their skills and diversity, they could play to large crowds in places like Riis Beach, and New York Coliseum as well as at schools and clubs.

If you were *good*, you might open for James Brown or Harold Melvin the way Flowers and DJ Hollywood did. If you had a distinctive style like Maboya's mix of reggae, funk and rock, you attracted devoted followers who came out every time you played. Crowds would follow you from gig to gig just like they did Pete DJ Jones. You might be known for your charismatic emcee who interacted with the crowd with slick talk between and on top of certain records.

You needed a great system that was not just loud. It had to be clear too. A crew was needed to help set up and carry equipment. An extensive record collection kept the crowd moving. It would come from different sources like Philly Soul standbys like *Love Is the Message*, *I Love Music* and *Bad Luck*. They could be funky instrumental breaks from rock records like Messina and Loggins' *Pathway to Glory*. Barabbas, an obscure band from Spain had joints like *Wild Safari* and *Hi Jack*---we rocked flutist Herbie Mann's version all the time in the park. Silver Convention's bass-heavy *Fly Robin Fly* and Crown Heights Affair's *Dreaming A Dream* were some other jams that were popular around our way.

Where I'm From: Growing Up Hip Hop

Radio played hit singles from the Jackson Five's *Dancing Machine* album, but DJs mined the album for treasures like *Mirrors of My Mind*. Some records were down-tempo, as low as 90 beats per minute. Others were mid-tempo or much faster. I watched DJs operate turntables like a gearshift on a sleek motorcar, taking me on a musical journey. To put things in perspective, it was like watching your favorite band or singer go to work. In New York City, there was nothing cooler than being a DJ.

Living in the city back in the 1970s was musically exciting. Although I grew up mainly around West Indians, Dominicans and Puerto Ricans were also rocking to music in the streets. Salsa and soul music were everywhere. Like signals from a cell tower, these sounds transmitted a powerful reception throughout the five boroughs. Joined at the hip, they formed a musical merger and it was called *Salsoul*. The music was well represented in every DJ's record collection. When we turned on our AM radios, we grooved to funk and soul on WWRL.

We were also up on the pop and rock broadcasting out of WABC. It was a joy sampling this sonic cuisine best served on 33 and 45inch platters. These aural appetizers and melodic main courses tantalized our adventurous musical palates. Turntables were the main ingredient that bounded these flavors together.

Just as our ancestors took what the slave master discarded and transformed it into something unique, DJs like my brother resurrected obscure records and gave them new life On certain records, they cut away the vocal fat and went straight for the meat which was the funky beat. Other joints like El Coco's *Let's Get It Together* featured sultry vocals that were welcome in our musical abode. The records we knew and loved rained down on park jams like manna from heaven.

Turntables may have been our weapon of choice instead of instruments, but we appreciated the musicianship that went into creating those records. Music was our passport to a world of pulsating African drums and breezy Latin rhythms. I could go on and on, but you get the picture. I will borrow the words from legendary radio DJ Frankie Crocker to sum up my recollection of this magical era; *It was the total Black experience in sound.*

The arrival of the 12inch single in 1976 changed everything. Before, DJs used two copies of a record to extend a break of a three-minute song. *Now* a record was five minutes or longer. It took up an entire side of a record and was mixed specifically for club use. Vocals were edited down, allowing DJs to manipulate the record anyway they wanted. Record companies provided DJs with promos---free records to break in the club. People would rush to record stores straight from the club to purchase what they just heard the DJ play.

Of course, DJs needed two copies. They either got them from the record labels or from a record pool. Dony belonged to the International Disco Record Center (IDRC). The IDRC was influential because it embraced non-white DJs, who were often excluded from this tight-knit club/DJ culture taking over the city. Dony had access to the latest records before they came out.

These extended versions had more space in the grooves allowing the record needle to move more freely during mixing. The sound was much richer, and the volume was much more powerful. South Shore Commission's *Free Man* and Double Exposure's *Ten Percent* was the first of these kinds of records.

Soon jams like CJ and Company's *We Got Our Own Thing and Devil's Den,* and Tom Moulton's remix *Love is the Message* were hitting the streets hard. You would never hear Don Ray's *Got to Have Loving* on the radio, but it was popular with us in the streets.

Besides playing in Brooklyn, Dony spun at events like Sunday Funday in 127 Park. The city closed the street off and amusement parks rides were brought in. There was food and the entire neighborhood came out. When my brother broke out *Soul Makossa*, the grooves and horn riffs cut through the muggy air like a knife through hot butter. No matter how hot it was outside, you *had* to dance.

Sound quality was key. So was ambience, lighting and equipment. The most important thing is your ability to play to crowds the way a singer or musician would. You had to know when to build up crowd intensity or bring them down. The blend had to be perfect between songs. So was timing. When that certain record dropped at the right moment, it threw the crowd into a frenzy. So could a rare song that no one had ever heard before. To master the art of moving the crowd, you needed skills and a great record collection. Not just the hits, but stuff that was not played on the radio.

In order to draw crowds and fend off competition, you might have to deconstruct or construct speakers to achieve the highest sound clarity. It might mean splurging on high-end Koetus Coralstone Platinum stylus needles made in Japan that cost three thousand dollars. For my brother, it meant hiring someone to construct a sound system. That was when he called Richard Long---the best in the game. He built the first outdoor mobile sound system for my brother. It sounded like it was made for a nightclub. Richard Long was instrumental in developing the proper atmosphere for music to be heard. He constructed bass cabinets and speakers. He understood that room design was critical to great acoustics in order to capture the perfect sound in a club.

Deejays were celebrities. Their signature playlists earned them hordes of devoted followers. They broke new records for record labels and made them hits in the streets before they even made it to radio stations. When radio programmers like Frankie Crocker came out to hear them and find out what was hot, that song would be on the radio the next day. Back then, elitist distinctions existed between club and mobile DJs. It was defined by race, venue and the type of crowd you played to. I am proud to say that Dony had his foot in both worlds too.

Dony Dancemaster

Where I'm From: Growing Up Hip Hop

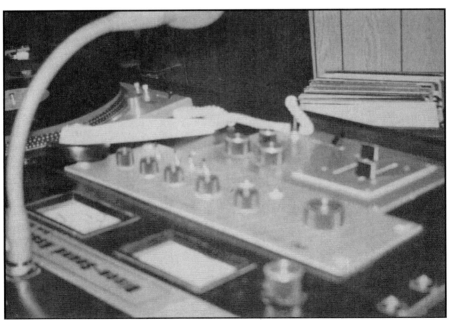

Where I'm From: Growing Up Hip Hop

Track Five

<u>No Idea's Original</u>

One of the reasons my man Hassan (Sonny) Pore and I made the *Founding Fathers* film was to shine the spotlight on the DJs around my way who paved the way for me. East Elmhurst's imprint in the game is strong. The Hurst's legacy is artistic flavor, musicality and sound. In our way we took it from the parks to the mainstream.

 Let me give you an example. Eric B and Rakim's classic *Eric B for President* is the epitome of East Elmhurst musical diversity. Smooth R&B and rugged soul co-existed like Poitier and Cosby. Rakim was not certain the mashup of Brown's *Funky President* and Fonda Rae's *Over Like A Fat Rat* would work. Thankfully his Hurst-born partner prevailed, and the rest was history. While some DJs brought house equipment out to play, King Charles used MacIntosh amplifiers to power music being played at our park jams.

 Dony's system was a Rolls Royce among a sea of Cadillacs. What makes him so special? For one---you had to have money. Two, you had to have access to the downtown movers and shakers. Three---you had to be good. My brother was all three! Dony was spinning at

Where I'm From: Growing Up Hip Hop

Manhattan upper crust disco Regine' while DJs from other areas played in school lunchrooms and gymnasiums. He was hired to play in clubs out of states.

No matter how you frame it, you cannot diminish the history---no contest! I am not trying to be elitist. Just stating facts. Stories about DJ Hollywood playing three clubs in one night are legendary. Before him, Chuck Berry traveled from gig-to gig with no band---him and his guitar. He would grab up whoever was around and do the show. Because these guys traveled light with no overhead, they were able to make more money. Dony's custom Richard Long setup gave him the best of both worlds---efficiency and quality.

Beatmatching and blending records were already done and perfected by downtown DJs before the uptown crowds ever got their hands on quality mixers. Before the usual suspects in hip hop folklore, there was Maboya---a one-man Mandrill and Caribbean force of nature rocking Panamanians, Trinidadians and Jamaicans. He made it cool to have eclectic sounds. You did not have to be from the islands to be able to catch the vibe but Maboya was ground zero for a West Indian DJ aspiring to get in the game like my brother.

Older cats like Hollywood, Pete DJ Jones and others are dismissed as "disco DJs" from critics playing records with similar tempos like Herman Kelly's *Dance to the Drummer's Beat,* Stephanie Mills' *Put Your Body in It*, Cheryl Lynn's *Got to Be Real* and Chic's *Good Times* for their DJ sets and rap routines. I got news for you*: if* *you're playing records for an audience, you are a "disco" DJ.* The term describes a certain type of music but at its core, it's really an alternative approach to delivering music outside of using live instrumentation.

The Hurst partied to so-called disco records, but we also got down to breaks like Babe Ruth's *The Mexican.* Before it became a park jam, it was already a staple downtown with The Loft dance crowd. The Incredible Bongo Band's *Bongo Rock 73* was in our DJ crates too. My brother, Nu Sounds and others were like magnets, drawn to the percussive sounds from the Motherland that existed in all kinds of records.

DJ Sesame from Astoria's Disco Twins used a term that encompasses the DJ's universal musical component: *ostinato*--- short melodic phrases repeated throughout a composition, sometimes slightly varied or transposed to a different pitch. In other words, loops. Samples. Pause taping. Catching the beat. It's all the same. We may not have known the word---*we just did it.* Black ingenuity is not exclusive. It's *inclusive.* Guys like KC the Prince of Soul and Nu Sounds may have not made it to the hot downtown clubs or became household names, but they were still founding fathers in *my* eyes.

Limited access to musical training in black inner-city schools is considered a reason why young people gravitated to emceeing and DJing instead of playing instruments. There were some exceptions. New York City's Princeton Plan consolidated schools to save money due to a deficit in the city budget, grouping schools by grade level instead of by the school districts they lived in.

Now education experiences were not restricted to schools in my hood. Black kids were bused to Jackson Heights and white kids were bused to East Elmhurst and Corona. A person might have spent their first three formative years in school in one neighborhood and then bused to another.

Imagine the culture shock. Junction Boulevard was the dividing line between East Elmhurst and Jackson Heights and the blacks and whites never mixed even though they live extremely close to each other. This would cause some racial tension behind the Princeton Plan. White parents were not too happy, but black students benefited from it. We received access to programs like pottery and cooking classes and music lessons. I was introduced to music theory and learned guitar. These lessons would pay off for me much later.

Where I'm From: Growing Up Hip Hop

Track Six
Booty Land and Beyond

127 Park was the heartbeat of East Elmhurst. People came from all over to hear great music. I could hear the thump of the bass rumble from blocks away. Dony Dancemaster, Nu Sounds or King Charles would pull up to 127 Park, unload the equipment, plug into a lamp pole and play. Bullet tweeters hung from the trees and the heavy bass bottom filled the park.

It wouldn't take long for people to start showing up. We had another name for 127---*Bootyland*. There were pretty girls everywhere, and they loved to dance. The set was fire. As soon as we heard the opening guitar licks from *The Mexican,* we knew it was on. The bass and drums had the crowd locked in a trance. Just as the song was fading, a familiar groove was building. Dancers caught the vibe and broke out into a six-step hustle. The park was really filling up now as the sultry vocals of El Coco's *Cocomotion* floated from the speakers. Jams like Tavares' *Heaven Must Be Missing an Angel* gave us a feel-good vibe.

Where I'm From: Growing Up Hip Hop

Over by the fence was Jeff Harris's frank stand. Cats stood in line looking to break the heat with an ice-cold soda. Sometimes they picked the wrong time to step off. I used to laugh when the brothers became possessed by the green-eyed monster watching their female dance partners hustle with someone else! There were great emcees too. Their style was basic back then. They hyped the crowd, but the DJ was the real star. If his system was powerful, he was the man. Even though the music was loud, our neighbors did not mind the noise---even when we partied until 3 am.

You could not miss a park jam. Kids would risk getting beatings if they stayed out too late. There was many a night an angry parent showed up at a jam, belt in hand, ready to lay out a teenager brave enough to stay out past curfew. Next week, they would be back at the park jam hanging out late as if nothing happened! I never had to go through any of that. Since I was around nine or ten, my parents would let me hang out with my brother till dark while he was jamming in the park.

The park was my center of the universe, year in and out. Bootyland was where you could always find me. There were other things going on too. Up the block from my house was St. Gabriel's on 98th street. It was a Catholic school where a lot of the neighborhood kids went. To make money, St Gabriel's rented out their basement for events. Our neighborhood mover-and-shaker Jeff Harris would book Nu Sounds, King Charles and my brother together for a battle of the

DJs bash. Sometimes he would book popular groups like Crown Heights Affair and Double Exposure to perform. These jams were for an older crowd, so I was too young to attend but I heard some great stories about these parties.

East Elmhurst and Corona are geographically linked. Both are only a half-mile apart, but they could not have been more different from each other. East Elmhurst was not as rough as Corona. The brothers out there seemed to think we were stuck-up and soft. Northern Boulevard was the dividing line. We attended the same schools and played in the same parks and shared all the local establishments, but the vibe was always territorial.

Whenever both hoods came together you could feel the tension in the air. If you ventured into Corona, you might get robbed. For some reasons, Corona dudes always wanted to fight us Hurst cats. Most hoods always had hard rocks---tough guys who had juice in the neighborhood. If you were nice with your hands you got respect. It was about your knuckle game.

Dudes were not into using guns yet. The only problem was the hard rocks *we* had sometimes held ourselves out to be for the other side of town, until you saw us headed back home before dark! There was one exception though. There was one goon that repped East Elmhurst to the fullest. While others were running to Corona for validity, he would hold it down in the Hurst. If anyone came to show out he would test them and shut things down. His name was Eddie

Where I'm From: Growing Up Hip Hop

Jackson. Eddie was a chubby little kid who grew up in the neighborhood and used to get teased and pushed around. After doing some time in the penitentiary, he learned the jailhouse and 52 blocks fighting style.

This kind of fighting was like martial arts or boxing, but it was done at the street level and taught in the jail system. While Eddie was away, he became a member of the Five Percent Nation and took on the name Everlasting. When he came home, he developed a reputation for knocking niggas out left and right.

Hard rock brothers had a certain mystique to them. They commanded your attention even if they were just chilling in the park, blasting *Apache* from a boom box when the DJs were not rocking the park.

They had style too. I can remember posting up at Bootyland with my crew when some hard rocks came to the park rocking straight leg jeans. We could tell from the white stitching and the horse on the back pocket they were wearing those designer Jordache jeans that we saw on TV commercials. *Designer jeans?* Please. Only GQ types or gay cats wore those. Plus, you had to have money. They cost *twice* the amount of our bell bottom Lees. It wasn't long before we switched up. Before you know it, the *entire* hood was rocking Jordache, Sassoon and Sergio Valente designer jeans!

Where I'm From: Growing Up Hip Hop

We also had righteous and spiritual brothers like High U Allah. We called him Hyulah for short. He was an older cat. Light skinned with a bald head like the actor Ji-Tu Cumbuka who played "The Wrestler" in *Roots*. This was a character that was strong and imposing who represented power and strength. "The Wrestler" was not on the screen very long, but his character made a lasting impression on me. I still remember the slave ship mutiny scene ending with his death from a cannon blast. He died on his feet instead of living on his knees as a slave!

Hyulah loved to play the drums and would set up in 127 Park during the jams. He never played along with the DJ so his drum sounds always clashed with the music and no one wanted to hear him.

One afternoon, when me and my crew were chilling in the park, Hiyulah rolled up on us like a force of nature. *"Let's take a ride."* Now we were in his car headed for southside Jamaica Queens. It felt like that carjack scene in *Cooley High*. Me and my crew were Cochise and Preach, riding shotgun with Stone and Robert, amped up over an unexpected and exciting interruption of our mundane routine. We just wanted to be down. We weren't on the Van Wyck Expressway five minutes before anticipation got the best of us. *"Where we goin?"* Hiyulah shut down our curiosity like that slave insurrection on Roots. *"Shut up and relax."*

We pulled up at a house. Inside, the vibe was serious. Almost mystic. The term *"Peace, God"* floated in the air like incense. I heard snatches of conversation from a few "gods" breaking down science and mathematics. We were given some literature called the Supreme Alphabet and Mathematics. I was a decent math student, but *this* was like nothing I ever heard before.

    We learned about how Clarence 13x Smith (they called him "the Father") broke away from the Nation of Islam to deliver teachings targeting the five percent or "poor righteous teachers" who lived among a "deaf, dumb and blind" eighty-five percent who were manipulated by a deceptive ten percent. My head was spinning. It was my first exposure to the Five Percent Nation of Gods and Earths.

Where I'm From: Growing Up Hip Hop

Track Seven

<u>Uptown Baby</u>

A rite of passage for a New York kid is that day you start riding the train alone. I relished the excitement at the thought of being able to spread my wings.

    The man who provided the passport to a world outside my window was Anthony Ruff. He lived in my neighborhood, but his grandparents owned a butcher shop in Harlem. On weekends, Anthony's parents sent him there to work and stay out of trouble. When he came back to Queens, he would bring back cassette tapes of DJs and emcees performing uptown. I recognized *Bongo Rock*, *Apache* and a few other records I had been hearing in Bootyland for years. The emcees were different. They were not just talking over records, they had *routines.*

    After I heard those tapes. I knew I had to travel across the bridge to see what was going on. I was in 7th or 8th grade when I started cutting class and jumping on the train with my crew; Ruff, Mark, Shawn, Larry, Benoit, and David.

Where I'm From: Growing Up Hip Hop

I couldn't skip school a lot, my parents did not play like that! They were into education. I hung with cats who were much smarter than me, so I was good. I could maintain without falling behind in my grades. I remember being so excited the first time I went uptown. The nervous energy I had was crazy! When we got off that train and headed for 125th street it was like we were in another world! I felt like Fred Williamson in Black Caesar walking down 1-2-5 with his crew to the sound of James Brown's *The Boss*.

It was like a dream come true. Everything I ever imagined came to life. I wondered if Auntie Irene felt like this when she first touched down in Harlem. I felt like Alex Haley in Roots, retracing the steps of my ancestors.

When we walked into a shoe store called British Walkers I was blown away. They had every kind of British Walker and Playboy shoe available. Leather. Suede. Every color you could imagine. These crepe-soled kicks were sooooo fly! Those joints felt like sneakers. There were so many Playboy flavors that you could coordinate them with your outfits.

Back in Queens, we were already matching up our nylon BVD t-shirts and boxers with our jeans, sneakers and Kangols. Now we could step things up a little. Everything still had to match but now you had British Walkers to rock with your jeans. Instead of a T-shirt, now you had a mock neck that matched your hat. A mock neck was a knit shirt that was almost like a turtle- neck but not as heavy. It was either short-sleeved or long sleeved. It gave your outfit a fly look while still being casual.

We would take the train to Delancey street to look at the sheepskin coats and the Kangols. We didn't have money so all we could do was window shop. Every time we hit Delancey, the response was always the same. *"Just wait til Christmas"* or *"I'm gonna be fresh on the first day of school."* We were gonna hit up our parents to buy us fly gear. When we got our bell bottom Lees, we had PC Kid, a local artist in our hood, spray our names in big graffiti letters on the legs.

I purchased most of my gear, but my wardrobe quickly expanded thanks to "five-finger discounts." We would walk into a store, grab three pairs of pants. Two would go in the jacket, another up the sleeve and we were out. I was lucky not to get caught. When we were not looking at clothes, we would head back to Queens and go to the airport. It was within walking distance from my house.

Back in the 70s it was very easy to move around airports. There were no security cameras, alarms or NTSA. You could just walk to the booth and cop a ticket with no crazy lines. The airport shops had all the latest eyewear like the Spalding aviator shades with mirrored lenses and the wrap around new wave joints. I would take 'em, two at a time. Today, it would be like walking in a duty-free shop and trying to walk out with bottles of top-shelf liquor. You could not do that now, but back then---it was soooo easy! We would shoot out to Jamaica, Queens and hit up the spot that would hook up our sweatshirts. They would iron our names on the shirt and add two playboy bunny logos on each side.

If I wasn't on the train headed someplace, I would be at Bootyland, with my friends showing off our latest gear listening to rap tapes and getting high. I was 14 years old having the time of my life.

Soon Afros are playing out and 360 waves are in. Out go the hot picks, blowouts and Afro Sheen. In comes the Dax and Nu Nile. I had the method down to a science. A couple dabs of "grease" on the scalp and throughout my hair. Hit it with the brush. Tie it down with the doo-rag to hold things in place. The next day I would go to school and the girls were seasick!

I took the high school entrance exam test to get into Art & Design in Midtown and I passed. I liked to draw and wanted to become an architect, so I was cool. Mark made it to Brooklyn Tech. Ruff got left back. Of course, I was fresh to def on that first day of school! I didn't have the *wack* wardrobe issues like I did years back. Everyone was styling and profiling. Walking through those halls that first day was like being on a runaway. Fresh Jordache and Puma sneakers, Adidas with fat laces, Lees in all colors and mock necks. Of course, it all I had to be color coordinated. Who knew years later that our style wars would catch on and spark hip hop fashion?

Where I'm From: Growing Up Hip Hop

It was about staying fly. If I had to take three trains and a crazy-long cab ride to some side street to cop the latest gear, I was always down. While kids my age were taking field trips to museums, we were exploring other hoods in Brooklyn, Uptown and the Bronx. I loved Manhattan the most. I wanted to be there as much as I could.

I made new friends from other boroughs but gravitated to the Harlem cats who played hooky and wrote rhymes all day. They showed me love and let me roll with them uptown. I wanted to soak up the action.

Art & Design had a lot of graffiti writers there at the time. I thought I was good until I realized there were a lot of cats that were much better than I was. I started to lose interest after a while. There were a lotta white boys into graffiti as well. They liked heavy metal guys like Ozzy Osborne but hated disco and rap. They wore sleeveless denim jackets with images of their favorite album covers painted on the back. They also wore "Disco Sux" buttons. We argued and debated whose music was best. Rock music was distorted noise to us. They didn't like DJ scratching and dancing was *not* cool. We spent our lunch breaks watching dudes from Uptown get down in the lunchroom. We formed a circle and cheered them on as they danced to the drummer's beat of their breakbeat tapes.

Every borough had a specific vibe that they represented. Uptown and the Bronx came with the hip hop energy. Brooklyn cats had hardcore street flavor while Queens was in the middle of it all, enjoying the best of both worlds. We were the common denominator because we had all the fly girls who dressed well and came from good homes. Brothers from the other boroughs always wanted to come to Queens to check them.

It didn't take long before I started slipping. In junior high, I was ahead of the curve when it came to the books. In high school I was behind the eight-ball. I racked up so many absences that the dean called my mother to come in for a meeting. Moms had to take a day off work and from the moment she showed up at school, everything slowed down like a dolly shot scene from a Spike Lee flick. As we sat outside the dean's office, I watched him slowly float toward us as he came down the hallway. He escorted us into his office and got straight to the point. *"Mrs. Lawrence, Ronald has missed 30 days of class this semester. We regret to inform you we have to release him. Effective today he is no longer a student here."* The dean's words were an endless loop on repeat in my head. I was crushed. I had embarrassed Moms. She was an honor student and a school teacher with a son who just got kicked out of school. Moms looked at me and burst into tears. My heart was so heavy it could have sunk in the East River. As Moms and I headed home, she painfully recounted her struggles, frustrations and embarrassment. It felt like a shot to the heart. Mentally, I started to blank out. I could see Moms mouthing the words, but now I couldn't hear her anymore. It didn't matter. The pain in her eyes said it all. I had stolen the best years of her life. *How could I be so selfish?*

Where I'm From: Growing Up Hip Hop

In that moment, I was Gator in *Jungle Fever* taking my mother's kindness for weakness. I wanted to fix things, but it was too late. Now I knew what Ruff must have felt like when he told his family he got left back. I ended up transferring to Bryant High School in Long Island City. I had gone from the penthouse to the pit. I felt like George Jefferson being evicted from that *de-luxe* apartment in the sky and having to go back to the projects. My adventurous spirit was curbed. For a while anyway.

Side II

My Mic Sounds Nice (1979-1990)

Where I'm From: Growing Up Hip Hop

Track Eight
<u>My Turn</u>

Soaking up the hip-hop creative energy going on around New York inspired me to get off the bench and get in the game. Of course, Dony was my inspiration. He was the first DJ I ever saw catch a break on turntables. It was 1976. Back then, Boz Scaggs' *Lowdown* was hot in the streets. I watched Dony work his magic, casting a spell over the park like voodoo. He went back and forth between two turntables, extending *Lowdown's* sharp drum pattern and throbbing bass. Dony was a sonic heartbeat pumping life into our park jam. It was a skill that he picked up back in 1974 while hanging at Promoters Manor in Flatbush, Brooklyn watching DJ Ron Plummer go to work.

When Kraftwerk's *Trans Europe Express* dropped a year after *Lowdown*, it sounded like nothing that was on the radio. I was becoming more intrigued with the sounds that made certain records hot.

The era before me was about what kind of speakers and amps you were using or what records you had. The DJ was the centerpiece.

Other elements moving to the forefront. It was about performance. Emceeing. Rhyming. Making beats.

I already had a head start thanks to the music lessons I learned in school. I smile when I think about it now, because subconsciously, I was following in my parents' footsteps when it came to making moves. They used past experiences as stepping stones and maximized opportunities around them.

My father's American Airlines job provided our large family opportunities to fly back to Dominica or give him and Moms a brief vacation. Moms was able to shape our formative learning years through her teaching gig. At some point most of us were students in her class. Now I was doing the same thing, channeling my musical experiences into this hip hop thing.

The transition from spectator to participant was complete the day when I heard a Grandmaster Flash cassette tape at 127 Park in '78. Flash was cutting up Juice's *Catch A Grove*. He stayed in the pocket, catching the song's drum and horn break. As soon as we heard Flash, my crew and I raided our parent's stereo equipment and started making pause tapes trying to outdo each other. We started building up our record collections. We would catch the train and hit up Downstairs Records. It was a small record shop tucked away on 42nd Street in the Times Square subway station around the E line. Since the 70s, devout emcees or DJs in the five boroughs made the pilgrimage to Downstairs Records to obtain that specific party rocker, classic or obscure joint that could light up a jam like the Fourth of July. If you were an aspiring crew like us trying to track down a certain break that we heard on a Flash or Cold Crush tape or if you needed that special sonic ingredient, *Downstairs Records always had the flavor you could savor, neighbor.* Elroy was our connect. He manned the store, pushing product on us young beat junkies. When we showed up, Elroy would reach for the racks of 45s behind him and pull out a record and put it on.

He played joints like The Soul Searchers' *Ashley's Roachclip* and Patty Lundy's *The Work Song*. They had the crazy breaks we loved. We hoarded our allowance money for weeks. Once we built up a nice stash, we headed back to the city to go buy records. Once we got home, we would locate the break and pause the tape. We would do this over and over until we had a hot beat to rhyme over.

Once we found out that Wally's Record Shack on Astoria Boulevard carried breakbeats, my crew and I were in heaven. We grabbed two copies of every record that we needed. *Sing Sing* by Gaz. *Daisy Lady* by 7th Wonder. *Ain't We Funkin' Now* by the Brothers Johnson. *I Can't Stop* by John Davis and the Monster Orchestra and *Rocket in the Pocket (Live)* by Cerrone. Now that we stockpiled our breakbeat arsenal, we needed emcee names to make the cipher complete. Mark became Wizard ME. Ruff was Spanky D. David was Davy D Well. Larry was DJ World and I was Ronnie Tuff. We called ourselves the B-Boys. We set up shop in Ruff's basement because he had a receiver and turntable. I brought over my parent's turntable so now we were good.

In the beginning we used the balance knob on the receiver to mix records until Mark got a Newmark mixer for Christmas. Mark and I went back to at least the fourth or fifth grade. The M.E. in his crew name stood for the initials of his name, Mark Eastmond. He would shorten it to DJ Wiz later. Wiz was smart but he was different from the average straight-A student. Wiz loved the street life and smoked weed from an early age. Besides being into hip hop, Wiz collected comic books and loved to watch wrestling on TV.

When Wiz got that mixer, it was big for us and solidified his permanent position in our crew. He was the one who stayed up on all the latest technology. Wiz was the first guy I knew in around the way with a computer. I never saw a floppy disk until Wiz showed me one. He would also teach me how to use an MPC-60 drum machine years later. It wasn't long before we graduated from the basement to neighborhood house parties. For now, we were the core unit. As time went on, we recruited other members into the group. Records like *Good Times*, *Ain't No Stopping Us Now* and *Bounce, Rock, Skate Roll Bounce* dominated the summer of '79 and we added them to our breakbeat collection. We would cut school and head over to Ruff's basement and practice cutting them up. Our turntables were not top of the line Technic 1200s. We had belt-drive SLB-100 models. In order to backspin, we had to place a piece of felt on the turntables to manipulate the records. We would also put a cushion on the turntable to stop them from humming.

I was the worst DJ in the crew. I was too heavy-handed. To be nice on the wheels of steel, DJs couldn't be clumsy. You had to have a light touch or else the records would skip. That was the last thing you needed when you were rocking a party. We would also put a penny or a quarter on the needle cartridge so it wouldn't jump.

As we worked on getting our weight up, we ruined a lot of records by trying to copy Flash's way of scratching records. He put his hand directly *on* the record to manipulate it back and forth. *"Ronald, what are you doing! No, do it like this!"* Dony screamed at me every time he saw me putting my fingertips on the record. Dirt and oil from my fingers would get on the vinyl. On top of that, all the weight I put on the cartridge would cause the needle to eat away the vinyl. You could have a great copy of a breakbeat but wear it out quick with a bad DJ technique.

The DJs from my brother's era had it right the whole time. When I saw other DJs go to work years later, I understood why they scratched with their fingers on the label. It took years of record abuse for me and my crew to get it right. I decided to stick with emceeing.

I didn't know it at the time, but I was also constructing the foundation for my future producing career. I may not have sealed the deal on the wheels of steel, but I had good ears. I didn't just focus on disco and funk breaks. I listened to the radio and paid closer attention to what was being played in the park. I also started going through my brother's record stash. Through my listening and digging, I was introduced to two records destined to change my life in the future: Herb Alpert's *Rise* and Chic's *Chic Cheer*.

Soon we got bold. Instead of being low-key and holing up indoors when we cut school to perfect our craft, we started hanging out at 127 Park. *Bad move*. Once Ruff's mother saw us and told my parents. I got an ass whippin.' While we were doing our thing, rap records had kicked off in a major way. During our trips to Harlem, I heard Spoonie G and Kurtis Blow blasting from Bobby Robinson's record shop. His record label *Enjoy* put out all the records that we loved like *Spoonin' Rap* and *New Rap Language*. It was one thing to hear records from your favorite emcee and another to be in the presence of a real live rap celebrity. I experienced *both*, thanks to Natalie Edwards. She was a girl from the neighborhood who lived a couple of blocks away from me on 99th Street.

Natalie knew that we were making a little noise in the neighborhood so she invited us to her house to meet her cousin who was visiting for the weekend. When she told us who it was, we knew we had to be there. Her cousin was Sha Rock from the Funky Four Plus One. They were one of the Bronx rap groups who made the jump from tapes to being on wax.

Where I'm From: Growing Up Hip Hop

While other emcee crews were mostly males, The Funky Four were like R&B groups Atlantic Starr and Rose Royce who had female lead singers. Sha-Rock was the centerpiece. They stood out. We had their record *Rappin' and Rockin' The House* in our crates. This shit was huge for us. To put this in today's context, it was like having an opportunity to chill with Jay-Z for a day. I was in awe. Sha-Rock was a nice emcee with a dope voice. Not only was she slender and cute, she was gracious enough to sign autographs and allow us to take pictures of her with our Polaroid cameras. Sha-Rock told us about a radio show on WHBI. The host, Mr. Magic played strictly hip hop and breakbeats. Groups would come through and do routines.

We would stay up late on Saturday nights hovering over our cassette decks with itchy trigger fingers ready to press the record button. Magic's show only came on once a week so I could not miss it. I would doze off sometimes but when I heard that familiar promo that kicked off the show, I was wide awake and captivated by the musical spell Magic worked on New York's super listeners.

Magic's intern, Jalil Hutchins created that dope promo. Jalil went from answering the phones to forming his own group, Whodini. A few years after they signed their deal, they became the first rappers to earn a platinum album. Their innovative production paired with Jalil's songwriting made them one of rap music's greatest groups of all time.

Where I'm From: Growing Up Hip Hop

When we weren't in the basement, we would be in 127 Park mimicking Busy Bee, Cold Crush and Fantastic 5 routines from the tapes Ruff brought back from Harlem. My man David from around the way had connections with Jamaicans in the neighborhood who owned a store on Astoria Boulevard that was a weed spot. They would always give him weed and David would bring us nickel bags. This became our routine---getting high and rocking those routines non-stop until the tapes popped.

"Ronald, do you wanna go to Harlem World with me? Beverly didn't have to ask me twice. She was just a year older than me, so she knew how much I loved hip hop. She was dating Vance, an older cat from Corona. Light skinned and stocky, Vance wore three-piece suits and sneakers.

We took a cab over to Harlem. As we headed over the bridge, it was hard to contain my excitement. Finally, I would get a chance to experience what I had been hearing on the tapes all this time. Harlem World's promoters Kool DJ AJ and RC booked a hot show. They were hip hop dudes, so they knew what time it was. AJ was one of the hot Bronx DJs I heard on the tapes. RC promoted many hip hop jams throughout the city. In the years to come, RC would make history as Van Silk, the man behind Rapmania, hip hop's first pay-per-view concert.

Rap music had only been on wax for a couple of years. There weren't many records, so the DJ mixed in R&B joints until showtime.

Where I'm From: Growing Up Hip Hop

People were just mingling, drinking and chilling. Suddenly, sharp keyboard blasts snapped the crowd to attention. Whether people were trying to get drinks at the bar or if they were in the middle of a conversation, when the first bars of the music hit, everybody rushed the dancefloor as if they were summoned by a mating call. The record moved the crowd like a park jam. For five minutes and change, a festive mood held the crowd in a death grip and refused to let go. When the DJ turned the sound down, the crowd sang the hook in unison, word for word. It was the first time I heard Frankie Beverly and Maze's *Before I Let Go*.

If high-profile groups like the Treacherous Three, the Sugar Hill Gang and Grandmaster Flash and the Furious Five were the NBA then Busy Bee, Cold Crush and the Fantastic 5 represented the more flamboyant ABA---flashy superstars whose exploits were witnessed only by those within the confines of the New York area. Their game was fan-tas-tic.

Now it was showtime! It was exciting to see these legends in action. It was like watching Jay-Z at Madison Square Garden. Their rap routines were intricate. Their vocals weaved in and out of the DJ's breaks like rush hour traffic. The delivery was rapid-fire, in perfect harmony and in key with the force of falling dominoes. Imagine the Jackson Five switching back and forth on that first verse of *ABC*. Now take that energy and flavor and multiply it by ten. *Then double it.* As DJ Charlie Chase cut up Cerrone's *Rocket in The Pocket,* the

Where I'm From: Growing Up Hip Hop

Headhunters' *God Made Me Funky* and Billy Joel's *Stiletto*, Cold Crush rocked the crowd with their legendary routines set to everything from Cameo's *Rigor Mortis* and WABC classics like Harry Chapin's *Cats In The Cradle* and Barry Manilow's *I Write the Songs*. I sang along as I envisioned myself onstage as the fifth emcee of the crew. *"It's us! You know it's us! the Cold Crush!"* I wanted to have the crowd in the palm of my hand the way Busy Bee did. I could not *wait* to get home and tell my friends.

On the ride back home from Harlem World, I silently basked in the afterglow of what I had just witnessed. I made a pact to never veer away from my hip hop path. I promised myself I would stay the course, no matter how rough the road got. When I got back around the way, lightning struck again.

"Check this out!" Ruff pulled out the latest tape he picked up in Harlem. The Furious Five were rocking a dope routine. As *usual* it was hot. *"Listen to this, just listen to this, for all ya'll emcees in a crew, this is what we want ya'll to do, shoo, shoo, shoo, shoo, shoo."*

I listened more closely. Something was different. The Furious Five weren't rhyming to breakbeats. *They were rocking to a drum machine.* My crew and I gathered around the boom box and lost our minds that day. It was something exciting about being pulled into this exciting world of beats and rhymes.

Where I'm From: Growing Up Hip Hop

Hip hop's sonic seduction was alluring, and we followed the music wherever it took us. Park jams. House parties. Train rides to all the boroughs. Downtown at the Roxy. The Disco Fever up in The Bronx. USA Roller Skating Rink in Queens. There were neighborhood fights and shootouts, but we didn't care. We just wanted to be part of the scene. To have that kind of freedom was liberating.

I remember coming home at six or seven in the morning and my parents never had a problem. It was just like my younger days when I could walk for blocks to hang out in another neighborhood and my parents weren't trying to keep track of where I was. Other times I would show up at a friend's door out of the blue and be welcomed in. Things are different today. There is no way I would give my kids the long leash my parents gave me.

I thought nothing could top Harlem World until I saw the Turnout Brothers and the Super Lovers perform at the Holiday Inn on Ditmars Boulevard. It was something special about seeing guys from the neighborhood doing this rap thing. Flash and Cold Crush were cool, but I wanted to be just like *these* dudes. An opportunity came sooner than I would expect. Bernard, the Turnout Brothers' leader was looking for replacements. In the streets, he was Original B or Rockin B, the hood legend behind The Turnout Brothers *and* The Super Lovers. Before that he was a leader of a crew called the Super 7. He was nice on the turntables. He was just as nice with his hands when it was time to knuckle up. He put the wheels of steel to the side and was now focusing on emceeing.

One day B saw me in the park and offered me a slot in the group. *"Ron, Cleve-o got caught up. He won't be back for a while. You wanna be down with us? You'll be a perfect fit."* I accepted B's invitation right then and there. From that moment, I walked through the door of opportunity and never looked back.

Where I'm From: Growing Up Hip Hop

Track Nine
<u>Step into the World of Ronnie Tuff</u>

When I hooked up with Turnout Brothers, I felt like a first-round draft pick. My stock shot up around the way. Instantly, I became a neighborhood celebrity. We needed a DJ, so I put Mark down. Six months later, Cleve reappeared.

I was amazed he got out so early. Cleve must have read my mind and answered the question in my head. *"My lawyer helped me beat the case because I was a juvenile, so I got off."* The lawyer who helped him out would become a great mentor to Cleve throughout his life. Later, he would end up becoming a lawyer. For now, it was about picking up where he left off. Cleve rejoined the group. Now it was time to get to work.

"Kid, stop telling jokes, let's do this, man! Wiz, do it again." From the corner of my eye, I saw Kid Coolout refocus on the task at hand. Kid was originally from the Bronx. He had a real fly rhyme delivery and an ill vocabulary. He was a great emcee and a dope writer. Kid was an intelligent guy. He had attended Bronx High

School of Science, one of the most prestigious schools in the city. He also went to Lehman College. Kid planned to pursue a law degree, but he put it on hold to pursue a career in rap music. Kid also had money. When his mom had passed, he came into some insurance money. He had a car before any of us and always rocked the flyest clothes. Original B was like Joe Jackson. A real taskmaster. Everything had to be just right. There was no room for slacking off. He would beat you down if you messed up. I always made sure I stayed on point. Remember that infamous Allen Iverson press conference where he brushes off *practice*? If B was coaching the Sixers back then, A.I. would be the *first* one at the gym shooting jumpers or running laps. B took no shorts and under his watch, we got good quick.

We rehearsed five days a week. Our routines and onstage movements were tight. I knew them like the back of my hand, but I still had a problem with crowds. I always felt like all eyes were on me, even when I stepped in the park or at the gym at St. Gabe's during a basketball game. I always got butterflies.

When we did our first show at Flushing High School, everything went smooth like clockwork. B's Joe Jackson power moves paid off. After the show, people really started to clock us around the neighborhood. I loved it. Especially when it was the girls. Whenever I would walk past them, the sound of their hushed whispers always caressed my ears. *"That's him. That's one of them Turnout*

Where I'm From: Growing Up Hip Hop

Brothers" I never had to introduce myself. No matter what I would go on to do later in my career, there was nothing like taking that hit of my first brush with fame. It was euphoric. Addicting. Every time I hit the park; I would hear voices saying *"that's Ronnie Tuff…"*

I might have been a hood celebrity, but I knew a cat who lived four houses down from me on 97th Street who was a real star in my eyes. He was a tall and skinny Five Percenter who called himself See Divine the Mastermind. See Divine and his partner Just Allah's World's Famous Supreme Team Show had rap fans all over the city listening to their show.

Back then, if you wanted to hear some hip hop on the radio, you had to stay up late to catch it. You didn't wanna play yourself and miss it. Otherwise, you had to go back to school on Monday and not be able to talk about the latest jam you just heard. The next time I saw See Divine I gave him a tape of our group. After he played it on his show, we started to get a little buzz around New York. Our rap routines became popular and cats in the hood started to recite them.

1982 was looking good. Five months after our first show, we heard there was going to be an emcee convention in September at Harlem World. We entered the contest. So did the Super Lovers. When we got inside the place was packed and star-studded. Doug E. Fresh. The Cold Crush Brothers. Busy Bee. The Fantastic 5. Dr Rock & the Force MCs. There were others on the bill too. They all were there for two things: win the cash prize and obtain emcee supremacy bragging rights.

We were dressed in our white stage outfits with our emcee names across the chest. Our tape may have given us a little buzz, but it was clear we were new jacks. We kept our cool and tried not to get impatient. It was one in the morning and we still hadn't performed yet.

The house emcee did some shout outs to keep the crowd pumped up. *"IS BROOKLYN IN THE HOUSE?"* BK was in effect and posse deep, holding the spot down as usual. You didn't wanna mess with them. The emcee went down the line. The Bronx, Manhattan and Uptown were representing and let everyone know it. By the time they got to Queens you could hear a pin drop. We were considered soft. Even the most thorough Queens dudes would have fallen back that night. They were not just out of their hood. They were out of their comfort zone and outnumbered. They did *not* want any static.

Suddenly, gunshots rang out and everybody broke north. Panic engulfed the room in a frantic embrace. A few people got stepped on. We headed for the emergency exit doors and ran out to the street. Once we all gathered together, we headed for the subway back to Queens. The Brooklyn kids swarmed the train station like wolves. They were wilding out, looking for people to rob. I saw them beat a kid down and take his Puma sneakers. As we rode home, the train was jam-packed full of thirsty dudes roaming the train cars looking for chains and purses to snatch. They overlooked us, but we were prepared to fight if we had to.

We went to WHBI a few times and linked up with The Supreme Team and started doing shows with them. Sometimes we did shows with Dr Rock and The Force MCs. We performed in Brooklyn, Queens, Mount Vernon, and other places throughout the city.

I was enjoying my notoriety, but I was ready to take things to the next level. I reached out to my brother Dony for help. When Dony worked at Regine's back in the 70s, he would rub shoulders with major people in the music business. He would always tell me about the TV stars, entertainers, record company execs and business moguls who came to the club. One time, he even brought back a signed picture of Michael Jackson for my sister Bernie.

One of the industry people who Dony was acquainted with was Cory Robbins. Cory ran Profile Records. He started out doing club music but after one of his acts, Dr. Jeckyll and Mr. Hyde dropped *Genius Rap* and it was a hit, Profile moved toward signing more rap groups. I never knew it at the time, but Cory also had a group from Hollis, Queens on deck who were destined to change the rap game forever. I got Dony to set up a meeting with Cory.

Normally, a manager coordinated label meetings on behalf of an artist. We were so new to the game that we did not even *have* a manager. We scheduled a meeting a few weeks later at the Profile offices on 57th street. I brought a cassette of our stage performances for Cory to hear. When he played the tape, he did not get what we were doing so he passed on the group.

Cory was looking for hit record potential and our routines didn't fit the bill. This was '83. Rap albums were just around the corner. The party-rocking style that was popular in the streets was fading. It might have worked three years ago, but now we were in danger of becoming casualties of a changing industry.

It was a lesson learned. Timing is everything in this business. It wasn't long before we broke up. Our last performance was at the Highlighters Club in Jamaica, Queens. It was a rap battle against a local group called the Rapmatical 5. The minute we got to the spot we felt the tension. When we went on, the crowd booed us. We were so rattled we could barely get through our routine. The crowd ran us out of the venue.

This was the last straw for B and Cleve-o. They had been with the group for a while and were ready to move on. I was just getting started and was ready to keep things moving.

While I was mapping out my next move, a guy from my neighborhood was making his. I lived on 97th Street. A couple of blocks from me were the Barriers, a family of three brothers who lived on 95th Street between 23rd and 24th Avenue. John was my age. He and I went to school together up until the sixth grade. The middle

Where I'm From: Growing Up Hip Hop

brother Anthony was known around the way as Ant Live. Ant was a dope graffiti artist who taught me how to write. He was a good emcee too. We called him Gangsta B. Ant didn't like his voice, so he fell back from the emcee thing.

Louis was the oldest. We called him Hook but he also went by his middle name Eric. He worked on a Mr. Softee ice cream truck and sometimes I would see him in the evenings on my street serving ice cream to the neighborhood kids.

Eric knew a DJ from over in Queensbridge Projects who was making a little noise. His name was Marley. Eric would roll with Marley to clubs in the city. Eric always carried a camera with him (like me) and took pictures of all the rappers. This was before paparazzi and bodyguards. Emcees were pretty much were local celebrities around the way and didn't mind letting you take their pictures. Eric carried these photos around everywhere he went and showed them off to his friends every chance he got.

One day Eric took me to Marley's apartment in Queensbridge. Hard drum sounds greeted us at the door when Marley let us in. Marley and his emcee Dimples D were making noise in the streets with a record called *Sucker DJs*. It had a similar drum pattern of a hot song bouncing around the city. It was in cars on the street. It was blaring from boom boxes in the park. The jam was called *Sucker MCs* from a new group from Hollis with a weird name---Run-D.M.C. Just beats and rhymes. No singing or routines.

Where I'm From: Growing Up Hip Hop

I remember Marley had the song's tape reel displayed on the wall over his Roland drum machine as if that joint was a priceless Basquiat or Andy Warhol painting!

Whenever I hung out at USA Roller Rink over in Jackson Heights, they played these songs a lot. The club was on 72nd Street and Roosevelt Avenue---not far from the Hurst. It was our local spot and all the major rappers would perform their hit records there.

Eric and Marley stayed in touch. A few years later, Eric ventured out to Long Island and linked up with an emcee from Wyandanch named Rakim. They would hook back up with Marley to record a couple of records that were game-changers. They changed it up business-wise too. A few years later, Eric and Rakim signed the first million-dollar rap contract and it was on after that. Next thing you know Eric's coming through the block with a Rolls Royce. He didn't just have one. He had two. It was a major step up from that Mr. Softee truck. *Way to come up, Eric.*

Knowing someone around my way trying to come up in this rap thing was motivating. It kept me inspired when things weren't working out for me. I didn't have to wait long for things to get popping. My next opportunity was right around the corner.

The Super Lovers had done some talent shows at the Disco Fever and other places. They had a buzz around the city. Now things were slowing down. Their leader, Herby Azor was looking to make changes. Herby lived in the neighborhood. We both shared Caribbean roots and I would see him in the park from time to time. Herby was an original member of the Super 7 with Original B. Now he had his own group. He offered me a spot and I took it.

My man Playboy was already down. Play attended Art and Design too but he was about 4 or 5 grades ahead of me. Play ended up getting kicked out of school like I did but he dropped out of high school altogether. I had known Play ever since I was nine or ten. He had a lot of street smarts that he picked up from his dad who was an old gangster and affiliated with the infamous drug dealer Nicky Barnes. Play may have been a high school dropout, but he was the sharpest one of all us. He had an entrepreneurial mindset. Like Herby, Play was also a trendsetter.

Years before Nipsey Hussle's community-minded power moves, Play created businesses in the neighborhood when he made it big. He had a barbershop and a clothing store on Astoria Boulevard within three or four blocks of each other.

Play really cared about his community. He kept the traditional East Elmhurst black business spirit alive. When guys like Dapper Dan and The Shirt Kings were breaking down doors when it came to hip-hop fashion, Play would do the exact same thing, designing custom gear at his IV Play store. He would also create a clothing line called The School of Hard Knocks.

Soon I was in the studio with Herby, Playboy, Quicksilver and Prince Charming to record *The Lovers Law*. It was in the vibe of records like *The Message* and *It's Like That*. Patrick Adams, the man behind so many of New York's great club records engineered the session and mixed the record. The record was a flop, but it didn't slow Herby down. He was driven and focused.

Herby had his own independent label, Quazar Records. He also had a home studio he called Noise in the Attic. Instead of blowing his money on clothes as I did, he bought equipment with the money he saved working the graveyard shift at McDonald's. He also worked another job at Sears over in College Point near Flushing. Even though we were known around Queens and we had a record out, things were not looking too promising. I kept the faith, thanks to a movie that I saw that changed my life.

It was the day before Thanksgiving. I was with my crew outside the Embassy 3 Theater on Broadway between 46th and 47th. We were waiting to see *Wild Style*, the first hip hop movie. My classmate put me on it. I knew her as Sandra from math class at Bryant High, but in the streets, she was Lady Pink, the legendary graffiti artist.

One of the few female "graf writers" at the time, Pink's vibrant art was everywhere. You saw it from a distance on trains crisscrossing the city or up close and personal in art galleries. Pink told me she was in the film. I didn't believe her until my crew and I got in the theater after waiting for hours in the cold---my mind was blown. *There she was!* Pink was not just an extra. She was a major part of the story. I was excited to see all the great emcee crews but when I saw Double Trouble, it was like I was on the screen. Just like Pink, they were around my age and suddenly, a career in hip hop seemed like it could be much more obtainable.

That winter I was hanging around Ditmars Boulevard with this short skinny kid named Alfred. He called himself MC Lil Man and he was down with a crew called the Super Rockin' Brothers. He had a partner named Steve Duncan who went by the name of Apollo. A tall kid named Todd used to hang around The Hurst from time to time---he had relatives or friends living there---he got cool with Apollo and Lil Man and they put him down with the crew. Todd had a reputation for walking around with a microphone in his back pocket.

Because I had some level of juice with the Turnout Brothers, Lil Man wanted me to come around to Apollo's crib to watch them practice in his basement. That was when I saw Todd for the first time. He wore a light blue Kangol and matching Puma sneakers. Todd loved the Cold Crush Four and was a big fan of Grandmaster Caz. As I watched them practice and write their routines in the basement, I noticed that Todd took the lead. They rearranged *Just Get On Up*, a Cold Crush routine set to the melody of Kraftwerk's *Numbers*. They added new lyrics and called their new routine *Our Shit is Crush*, repeating the chorus throughout the beat. When Todd introduced the crew members in a rhyme, he used his emcee name---Cool J.

Later that night, Herby came through. He joined Apollo, his girl and me as we walked Todd to the 7-train station on 103rd Street because he had to get back home. We looked out for security as Todd hopped the turnstile and headed back to Farmer's Boulevard. Back in the day we were not rolling with a lotta money, so we hopped the turnstile every chance we got. We would rather spend seventy-five cents on chips and a soda instead of train fare. If there were cops around, sometimes we would still hop the train anyway.

A year later, I was listening to the radio and I heard a familiar voice. *"I need a beat/Farmer's Boulevard/ladies love Cool J!"* Herby later told me that this was Todd---- the same kid we walked to the train station a year ago. He was now calling himself LL Cool J. Instantly, I became a fan. When Herby and I went to see LL perform at the Roxy, some dudes in the crowd kept interrupting his set which pissed him off. After the show, LL had beef with some cats who met him in the men's restroom and wanted to fight him.

When I saw that LL had made his dreams come true, it gave me the drive to keep pushing forward as an emcee.

Where I'm From: Growing Up Hip Hop

Where I'm From: Growing Up Hip Hop

Where I'm From: Growing Up Hip Hop

Original B, Ronnie Tuff and DJ Wizard M.E.

The Kid Coolout and Cleveo the Rockchild

Where I'm From: Growing Up Hip Hop

Turnout Brothers, Circa 1982

Where I'm From: Growing Up Hip Hop

Herby Luv Bug and Ronnie Tuff

Where I'm From: Growing Up Hip Hop

Chapter Ten
Idol Maker

It is 1985. Herby is still at McDonald's and Sears. He is also enrolled at the Center for Media Arts in Manhattan. Kid is at Sears with him. His girlfriend Cheryl James and her homegirl Sandy Denton work there too. They worked as telemarketers selling customers equipment and parts' warranties for their appliances.

It seemed like everybody from the neighborhood worked there at some point. Play and I worked there for a minute until we got fired. Everyone in our circle was from East Elmhurst except Cheryl and Sandy. They were from Jamaica, Queens. Another cat who came up from Maryland worked there for a while. His name was Martin Lawrence. When he was not working at Sears or the Hess gas station across the street, he was in Manhattan trying to get his comedy career off the ground.

As we worked our nine-to-fives, Doug E. Fresh partnered up with my sister Bernie's old Music and Arts schoolmate Ricky D and made a record called *The Show*. It had the flavor of the old rap routines, but contained vivid storytelling. I did not just hear the record. I could also literally see what was going on. It was not the aggressive Run-D.M.C style that was popular at the time. You could dance to it plus it was a great radio record.

Built around a rap concert concept, Doug and Rick moved seamlessly from backstage banter to slick narratives. Doug was the human beatbox who played straight man to Rick's comedic cavalier cool. When I heard Doug mimic telephone and drum sounds like Ralph MacDonald's *Jam on The Groove* percussion break, it sounded like the best record I had heard in my entire life. The joint moved Herby too. He was putting together a music project for school and he toyed with the idea of putting together a female rap group. At that time all the hot rap artists were males.

Herby was ahead of the game with his vision. He already had a name for the group---- *Super Nature.* He took it from Cerrone's disco breakbeat jam that we used to rock at 127 Park. My sister Bernie, her best friend Crystal and my high school girlfriend Tarsha were the first incarnations of the group. Herby wrote their rhymes and they practiced in my basement.

It didn't last. They were all focused on going to college. Bernie was looking forward to going to Howard University. Herby wanted her to be the DJ, but my parents would have been against Bernie terminating her studies to pursue a career in music. Herby didn't think it was practical to create a group around three high school girls planning to move away. He replaced the girls with Cheryl and Sandy.

Herby still needed a third member and he still thought that Bernie could be a dope DJ, but she was adamant about not letting my mother down so her decision was final. Herby found Latoya Hanson in the Bronx. He named her Spinderella. Herby had finally found his group.

He came up with the idea to record an answer record to *The Show*. He called it *Show Stoppa*. It was a great idea. Marley already had done it with his emcee Dimples D and Roxanne Shante who blew up with her own answer record to UTFO's *Roxanne, Roxanne*. Herby used his sampler to hook up a beat. He groomed and coached Cheryl and Sandy in his attic. Once they had the rhymes down pat, he booked studio time in Long Island City at Power Play Studios using the money he saved from his jobs.

When the record was done, Herby pressed it up and took it to WBLS where Marley Marl worked with Mr. Magic. When the record took off and became a hit, Herby finally quit both of his jobs. He was now a hit producer with a hot group. It was exciting to see things happen for Herby. He was light years away from that cat clashing with Original B over the direction of the Super 7 emcees. Now he had his own thing. After *Show Stoppa* hit, Herby parlayed it into an album deal for Cheryl and Sandy with Next Plateau Records. He ditched the

Supernature name and came up with a new name, pulled from a lyric that the girls had kicked----*Salt N Pepa.*

When people talk about hip hop and R&B cliques that made noise in the industry, Herby doesn't get enough credit. Herby was before his time. He had a millionaire mind and was all about being independent. His thing was, rather than go to someone else, the crew should be doing it ourselves.

Herby was wise enough to realize that he could pocket his production budget money by building a professional studio in his garage. Instead of passing his groups over to Russell Simmons' Rush Management like everyone else, he went on his own. Salt N Pepa were one of the few female acts during the male-dominated rap scene at the time. They stood out for many reasons. They were a female group with great voices. Their records were dope and they were fine.

Cheryl and Sandy were the total package. They hit the industry just as more and more record labels were funding rap videos for their artists. When Salt N Pepa's videos started to hit, they attracted male and female fans. Because they were fly, brothers liked them. Because they were emcees, the ladies looked up to them. Other females wanting to get in the rap game were also inspired by the group. They were the cornerstone of Herby's emerging empire and Russell wanted them.

Where I'm From: Growing Up Hip Hop

I was at Herby's house the day Jam Master Jay pulled up to the curb in a dope black Jeep 4x4 with his girl. They both were rocking custom leather Louis Vuitton outfits from Dapper Dan.

During this time Run-DMC was on top of the world. Behind the scenes, Jay was also instrumental in the success of Def Jam and Rush Management. He could produce and he had an eye for talent. He was great at putting people together. Jay got straight to business. *"Ya'll should be down with us! Salt N Pepa are dope. They need to be with us. Let's get this money!"* Herby didn't budge. He had a member of the biggest group in hip hop in his living room extending an invitation to be down. It was like Jay-Z asking him to join Roc-A-Fella Records.

Herby stuck to his guns. Instead of signing Cheryl and Sandy over to Rush Management, he created Idol Makers Management and became Russell's *competitor*. Russell didn't speak to Herby for years. Back in those days, Russell had a monopoly on the rap game. All the major tours came through him. If you were not "rolling with Rush," he would try and shut you down. Herby found a way around all that. He got the Salt N Pepa on great tours. He pushed back against the mighty Rush empire to do things on his own terms.

One night I went to check Herby at his attic studio. He had just bought a Roland 808 drum machine and was very excited about getting to work. He wanted to make a song like LL's *Rock the Bells*.

Where I'm From: Growing Up Hip Hop

I used my mouth to create drum snares and Herby programmed the beat into the drum machine.

When I heard the finished track, I was blown away by Herby's genius. He added more samples and sound effects to fill out the track. Cheryl and Sandy's flow were on point. Herby had taken my drum pattern idea, built a full composition around it and transformed it into a masterpiece. He called it *I'll Take Your Man.* Herby was also working with a Brooklyn rapper named Dana Dane whose first single *Nightmares* was becoming a hit. Herby was on his way to building an empire.

Herby came a long way in a short period of time. I remembered the days when he was just finding his way as a producer. Just a couple years ago, rap records were moving away from the old Sugar Hill sound to jams like T La Rock's *It's Yours* that paired hard drum sounds with complex lyrical deliveries. These songs were influencing the production style of the next wave of rap records. Over in Queensbridge Projects, Marley liked the beat so much that he recreated the song's whole sequence pattern. Because he had a Roland TR808 drum machine, he was able to replicate the entire song.

Herby looked up to Marley and was eager to soak up any information regarding beat making and production. We went out to Marley's to see him. When we got there, Herby noticed Marley's sampling machine. It was so small it could fit in the palm of his hand. It was an Electro Harmonix Instant Replay digital recorder that record sounds and manipulate sampled loops. It also had the ability to slow them down or speed them up. The recorder had sampling capability that was only about a second long.

The most you could probably get out of it was a kick and snare from the sampling time. I was bugging out about how so small a machine could help create such big sounds.

"That's the equipment that Marley made Marley Scratch with." Herby picked up on it immediately as he referred to a big beat jam that was beating the old school sound into submission. After Marley provided a demonstration, Herby went out and found his own. Now he was able to step his game up.

Word got around fast. Ant Live showed up at Herby's crib with an emcee named Abdul who lived down the street from me on 93rd Street going down towards Astoria Boulevard. He went to St Gabe's Catholic school when he was younger. They called him Dule. Ant knew Herby had a small studio setup in his attic bedroom of his parent's house. He always had a beat ready for a good rapper to spit to. Herb cued up the beat and he and Dule went back and forth on the mic. Dule had an aggressive style and a witty swagger when he rhymed.

Dule strung his words together like pearls on a string. It was like he never took a breath. He had a lisp, but you could still hear every word he said. I could tell he was gonna be big. It was my first time witnessing the greatness of an emcee who called himself the Kool Genius of Rap. Just like Eric, *Kool G Rap* would hook up with Marley to become one of rap's great heavyweights and influence future cats like Nas and Big Pun.

A lot had happened in these last couple of years. Herby did not want to be part of Super Lovers anymore. He saw his future as a record producer. My guys Kid Coolout and Playboy got together and formed a group called the Fresh Force Crew. They had a good relationship with a WBLS DJ named Charlie Casanova who started working with them.

During the Sugar Hill/Enjoy era, live musicians replayed the hottest breaks for emcees to rap over in the studio. Now, whenever a hit song with a funky beat came out, emcees raced to the studio to record a rap version on the heels of the original.

Charley Casanova wanted to make a rap version of Falco's *Rock Me Amadeus*. He put together a track replaying the beat and added a guitar that copied Led Zeppelin's *Who Lot of Lovin'*. He dispatched Kid to find a good emcee to round out the group. Kid pulled me in and literally the next day we were in Long Island City at Power Play Recording Studios.

This was the moment I'd been waiting for. My dream was in my grasp! This could be my big break. I was so nervous but found a way to pull myself together. After finishing the hook and the verses,

Where I'm From: Growing Up Hip Hop

Charlie Casanova did not care too much for my voice, and he passed on me.

The guys ended up finding a rapper out of New Jersey named Kasim. They ended up getting a deal with Sutra Records and putting the record out. I felt like I was running out of time. It seemed like *everybody* in my neighborhood was making moves but me. Kid Coolout and Playboy had joined forces as Fresh Force. Herby, G Rap and Eric B were making moves in the music business. My rap career seemed like it was over. I was feeling left out. It was time to make my own moves.

For the past two years, I had been taking courses at the New York City College of Technology in downtown Brooklyn. Now it was time to make some permanent decisions that would set me up for the future. I applied to other colleges out of state.

I received an acceptance letter from Howard University that summer, but I still was not sure what I was going to do. I waited for the last minute to make my decision. Two weeks before the first day of school, I told everyone I was leaving for college. They were in shock. I was not sure how things would turn out, but it was time to leave East Elmhurst.

God bless my family. Even as I drifted and tried to stay afloat, the examples they set were a guiding light. They always supported me and never let me down. My sister helped complete the transfer paperwork. I had never left New York City to travel to another state except for New Jersey. I would travel back and forth to the West Indies but that was it. Life's new chapter was waiting. I was DC bound!

Where I'm From: Growing Up Hip Hop

Track Eleven
Howard, Hip Hop and Herby

Harlem may have been the Mecca for style and flavor, but DC was ground zero for cultural enrichment back in the eighties. Howard was the premier historically black college and it seemed like every young black person in the world was there. The intoxicating scent of Black pride was everywhere. It radiated from the faculty to the students. Because certain family members went to Howard, I was vaguely familiar with the school. What I was not prepared for when I landed on campus was my cultural transformation.

All my credits didn't transfer over so instead of continuing my studies in architecture I wound up pursuing a degree in liberal studies. I also received a different kind of education. After hitting the streets and soaking up what DC had to offer, my favorite spot quickly became a bookstore up the street from the campus on Georgia Avenue. It was called Pyramid Bookstore. I called it The House of Knowledge.

I would go there often and purchase lots of books. The first book I got my hands on was a book called *Malcolm X on Afro*

Where I'm From: Growing Up Hip Hop

American History. It triggered an unquenchable thirst for knowledge and the impact was immediate. I went from being informed and enlightened to becoming *inspired*. My spirit and soul were rejuvenated. Just as Bruce Lee suggested, I became like water, shaping myself into a holistic transformative image. I changed my diet and became a vegetarian.

It wasn't long before my newfound spirituality and sense of purpose would be tested. During summer break, I worked at a video store on Astoria Boulevard on 93rd Street for the summer break. VCRs were popular and just about everybody had one.

A lot of people in the music business would come to the store to rent the latest videos. I would see G Rap's partner DJ Polo and R&B singer Glenn Jones---he rented an apartment from Kid Reid's father. LaLa Cope a songwriter with the Hush Productions R&B team was from the area and she would also come through. Her colleague Wayne Garfield came around too. They worked behind the scenes with R&B/dance band Change on records like *Searching* and *The Glow of Love*, that I loved so much. Seeing all these music people was just like living *The Godfath*er's Michael Corleone character in real time: *just when I try to leave, they pull me right back in.*

I was just getting comfortable with my hiatus from music but my constant interaction with industry people had me rethinking my decision. Maybe it was a sign.

Where I'm From: Growing Up Hip Hop

One day Kool G-Rap and his friend Shannon came by to rent videos. Shannon took one look at me and fell on the floor laughing. G didn't say a word. As Shannon got himself together, he sneered *"so this is what you're doing now?"* I guess he felt I had fallen off after my run with the Turnout Brothers.

I just took a different route and chose to pursue education. There was no guarantee I would even have a music career. Until I could figure out where this music thing was going, school would have to be my way out. To me that was a logical move. To Shannon, I was over. As he kept laughing, I smiled along with him and got the videos they wanted.

As I walked through the Howard campus for the first time, the first thing I noticed was the women. They seemed to be everywhere. The ration was about 18 to 1.

New York sisters had that edgy flyness I knew so well. The southern girls were not as aggressive, but they had a unique vibe that sparked my curiosity. East Elmhurst was known for their women, but this was something else. I loved it. When I went off campus to hang out, I saw the freshmen wopping it out to my man Hook's two-piece combo, *Eric B is President* and *Check Out My Melody*. The upperclassmen were feeling house music more than rap. Instead of LL or Eric and Ra, Colonel Abrams was king. I also got exposed to go-go music. DC cats liked it better than rap. The music was heavy on horns and drums. Cats did chants, hooks and some call and response---a little like emceeing. Super basic. I wasn't feeling it as much and it took a while for the music to grow on me.

The slang took even longer. DC did not have boroughs like New York so when a cat said he was from *"soufeas'* or *"norfeas"* I did not know what the hell they were talking about. The first time a DC cat greeted Me with *"whassup, shorty?"* I felt disrespected. That's what we called women up in New York. Every other girl was from *"PG."* Once I was standing next to a sister (*yeah she was from PG too*) and heard her whisper to her homegirl, *"girl look at him. You know he a bamma."* One time a go-go jam was playing on a boombox and a brother said *"that JONT slammin', Joe."* Another kid told me I was "lunching." It was like I was dropped off into another universe.

Now I saw why most New York students rarely ventured out into the city. They basically stayed on campus. All the New York freshmen stuck together. We gave off a vibe that radiated from us like an exotic scent. Our fashion, slang, dance and music made us stand out from the crowd. Collectively we had juice but alone, I was just a new face in the crowd. For the first time, no one knew who I was. I went from neighborhood rap star to just Ronnie Lawrence. It felt like I was starting all over again. I started entering talent shows held at Crampton Auditorium. Between classes and homework, I was writing rhymes every chance I got.

Where I'm From: Growing Up Hip Hop

Back home, Herby was still working on Salt N Pepa's album. I kept up with his progress by telephone. During that time, the Junkyard Band had a double-sided single record out that was rocking DC. The B-side of the record---*Sardines* was hot, but I fell in love with the A-side too. It was called *The Word*. It had a vibe of old New York "state of the world" records we were doing a few years back. It had a funky go-go drum break that I fell in love with. I bought the record and sent it to Herby.

He used it to create *My Mike Sound Nice* for Salt N Pepa. Herby was also working with Dana Dane, an emcee from Brooklyn. He went to Music and Art with my sister and rapper Slick Rick. He had blown up with *Nightmares* and now Herby was producing his first album. Over the phone, I created bass lines and drums sounds with my mouth that Herby programmed into his drum machine. It was the foundation for *Keep the Groove*. It made the album and Dana gave me special thanks for contributing. It was the first time I received any type of album credit and it felt good.

It was great to be recognized but I didn't want to produce records. I could care less about a drum machine. I wanted to have a hit song of my own on the radio. Nothing else mattered. Things were picking up though. I got a call from Herby. He was really rolling. His deal with Next Plateau Records provided him with an opportunity to make a compilation album. He called it *Hurby's Machine*. He changed up the spelling of his name and it looked fly. It was like his alter-ego. Hurby was really carving out an identity for himself as a super producer.

He had an idea to put two members of the crew back together to make a record. Sundance and I were the last two members of the Super Lovers---the odd men out from a crew of emcees and DJs who were already in the game. I appreciated Hurby for putting us down. *Let the Drummer Get Ill* was not a hit but the song's pounding drum sounds made it one of the hardest tracks on the album. Herby used a couple of samples from The Meters and programmed a beat that sounded like James Brown's *Funky Drummer*. The first time I heard the track, it felt like a shot of adrenaline. I was charged.

When it was time for me to say my verses, I was ready. Years of pent-up frustration had my heart beating like a kick-drum. I closed my eyes for a second and every emcee moment I experienced flashed in front of me like rolling film credits or vivid outtakes of movie scenes. Extreme wide shots of Harlem World. Panned medium shots of Cory at his desk, shaking his head in rejection. These vivid reminders jolted me back into reality. *"Let's go, Herby. I'm ready."* I pushed the headphones closer to my ears and I went for mine: *let the drummer get ill/so let it shall be done/like Moses the prophet/I'm the chosen one!*

On the strength of that song I got my first interview in Howard's newspaper, The Hilltop. They did a write up on me, promoting the song's release. Just like that, *I was back on!*

Where I'm From: Growing Up Hip Hop

Now It's '87 and Herby is *really* killing it. He's not just Herby from Queens anymore. Now, he was *Hurby Luv Bug*---super producer-slash-manager to some of the hottest rappers in the industry. He has a kitted-out red Benz 190 now.

Hurby's Machine did okay. *Dana's Dana Dane with Fame* did even better. It was on its way to gold, thanks to hit singles *Nightmares, Delancey Street* and *Cinderfella Dana Dane.* Salt N Pepa's *Hot Cool and Vicious* was already gold, when a B-side called *Push It* started getting radio airplay it pushed *Hot Cool and Vicious* over the platinum mark.

Hurby's product was flooding the streets and when it was time to re-up, he gave me a package of my own. It was like a scene from *Superfly*. I was Priest to Hurby's Scatter who was offering me a scholarship. *"You have good ideas, instead of giving them to me, why don't you just create a beat by yourself? "I'll put it on the album, and you'll get royalties for it."*

When I went home for Thanksgiving weekend, I got with my boy Wizard M.E from my old crew. Wiz was still on his equipment game. He had an MPC-60. Wiz only stayed a few doors down from me. When I showed up at his house with an armful of records, we got to work. I told Wiz how I wanted the beat to be structured. He listened to what I had, followed my instructions and made the beat. I took it to Hurby, and he used it for Salt N Pepa's second album, *A Salt With A Deadly Pepa*. The song was called *Hyped on The Mic*.

Where I'm From: Growing Up Hip Hop

Back at Howard, I was getting a name for my hip-hop affiliations. Rap videos were popping up more. People were starting to see what their favorite rappers looked like. When I pointed out certain artists I knew, no one believed me. When I pulled out my photo album, they started believing the hype. It was like I knew Michael Jackson.

I stumbled on hip-hop photography by accident. I was tagging along with Hurby, Kid and Play with my camera and I was getting to meet a lot of the rappers in the clubs and take pictures of them. You rarely saw photographers roaming around the club at the time. If you saw one, they were doing it just for fun. I was doing it to show off to my friends back at Howard. I had accumulated two fat books of pictures and people would come to my dorm room to check them out. My dorm room was like a museum. I had no idea I was documenting history. For me, photography was a hobby. I was doing it strictly for enjoyment.

Back in the 80s, radio and club airplay were critical if you wanted your records to pop. Red Alert and the Awesome 2 were DJs at the New York's The Latin Quarter (LQ). If they liked your song and played it; you were good. Herby would bring Salt N Pepa. They were the only female rap group in the clubs, so they stood out and got plenty of attention. Kid N' Play were also on the scene promoting their records.

You had to be bold to rock gold at the Latin Quarter. It was a sign that you made it or had a little dough. Gold jewelry also made you a target. If "Dog" from Brooklyn was in the house, you knew shit was gonna go down.

One night I was hanging at the LQ with Herby and his brother Steve. He wore a fat rope chain around his neck. Steve rocked a gold bracelet on his wrist. I could feel the tension in the room. The music was loud, the club was dark and filled with smoke. A posse of dudes appeared out of nowhere and moved closer to us like zombies from *Night of the Living Dead*. They formed a tight circle around us, sucking out our party vibe like a vampire. BAM! A fist knocks me to the ground and sneaker soles are headed for my cranium. I cover up as best as I can. Now they are gunning for Hurby's chain. He had a death grip on his jewels and tried to fight back, but the force of the blows was too much for him to handle. When the chain popped from around his neck, Dog and his posse melted away in the crowd. No matter how hectic it got, we always went back.

Rakim at the Latin Quarter

Salt n Pepa at the Lartin Quarter

Where I'm From: Growing Up Hip Hop

Heavy D and friends at the Latin Quarter

Biz Markie and friends at the Lartin Quarter

Where I'm From: Growing Up Hip Hop

In Eric B's dining room (Bernie, Kid and Eric B.)

Kid n' Play

Salt n Pepa at the Tramp video shoot

Where I'm From: Growing Up Hip Hop

Dana Dane and Jam Master Jay

Chuck Gillout and DJ Run

Where I'm From: Growing Up Hip Hop

Hanging out in Eric B's living room

Play, Red Alert and Kid at the Latin Quarter

Dana Dane with friends at the Latin Quarter

Hanging backstage with Mike Bivins and Heavy D

Where I'm From: Growing Up Hip Hop

Eric B and Rakim

Where I'm From: Growing Up Hip Hop

Where I'm From: Growing Up Hip Hop

Fresh Prince (Wil SMith) and AMEN-RA

Chris Rock, Amen-RA and Kid

Trouble T-Roy and I

DJ Wiz, Play, Quicksilver and Kid

Where I'm From: Growing Up Hip Hop

Track Twelve
<u>Puff</u>

One day, a skinny browned-skin brother rolled up on me when I was on campus. His name was Sean, but they called him Puffy. He heard out about my Hip Hop photo album and wanted to check it out. He showed up at Sutton Plaza and found me chilling in my room. As he viewed my portfolio, he told me that he had never been inside of a recording studio before. *"Yo, these are some dope pictures. Can I hang out with you some time and check out some clubs?"* As we talked, I learned he was from Mount Vernon. When he said that, I paid a little more attention.

He and my brother lived five or six houses away from each other. When we would go home on school vacations, I would take him around to places where my friends in the business were performing. Once I took him to a Kid N' Play session at Bayside Recording Studios in Queens.

It was Puff's first experience witnessing a recording studio session, but it would not be his last! He returned the favor by offering to show me the spots where he would cop his fashionable gear during our next summer break. I picked up Puff and his man Groovy Lou and we headed for the city. When we got to the Village, we hit up some jewelry spots. I picked up a couple of small chains. I was feeling good about my purchases until Puff brought me back down to earth. *"Yo ha, why you wasting all that money on jewelry when you can buy more clothes with that. Get the wardrobe together first playboy! Look at me ha, even in my bummy clothes I still look fly!"*

Puff had on his signature black Reebok sneakers. Even in jeans and a t-shirt, he looked smooth. He took me to his favorite spot, Le Chateau. I believe Uptown Records artists wore their clothes and it was also the place where all the Mount Vernon cats would buy all their gear. It was a slick style, Puff and his friends made popular at Howard. They wore stuff like baggy linen and rayon pants in multiple colors with floral print shirts. Cats would also rock clownish-looking kicks we called bump toes, a cross between a dressy and casual clown style shoe.

I wasn't interested in that style. I liked a more toned-down look. I was a hip-hop dude, but I didn't mind rocking some GQ shit every now and then for the ladies on campus. Puff was a master of that fashion shit and he put me on to some gear. I was ready to head back to Howard in style. I stayed with Derickson during my breaks. In the summer, I worked an assembly line job at General Motors in Tarrytown so that I had some paper for the rest of the school year. I wanted to build my credit, so I copped an American Express card. I used Pops' old Plymouth Horizon to get back and forth.

Puff and I hung out a few times on our breaks when we would come home. We would hit a few clubs and I would bring him around to see G Rap and Kid N' Play perform. I was proud of my brothers. From the ashes of my old Turnout Brothers and Super Lovers crew, those two cats rose like a phoenix to become another critical piece of the East Elmhurst hip-hop family tree.

Kid N' Play had great chemistry like Run and D. Kid had the ill flattop. He had the lyrics. He could be funny or come hard with battle rhymes. Play was smooth. He was the ladies' man with a conversational flow. Very stylish. They were good dancers too. Hooking back up with Hurby as a duo was a smart move. They blew up fast. In a few years, they would conquer radio, TV and film. They were not just a rap group they were a *brand*. Kid and Play would move hip hop into a commercial space very few ever would touch.

When the Awesome Two threw their annual summer parties out in Jersey, we were there. Puff was anxious to soak up everything hip hop. Because of my connections I was always willing to oblige. He was always ready for anything. One time I was in Queens getting ready to roll out with Kid and Play for a show and Puff was nowhere to be found. I called his house *"Yo, you need to be here in the next twenty minutes or niggas is gonna leave us. These Kid and Play dudes are never late for shows They're not gonna wait for me!"* Just like clockwork, I see Puff's black Volkswagen Cabriolet headed toward me at top speed. Puff was never going to miss an opportunity.

Puff was always ready to make moves. The more I hung with him, he made his aspirations known. He had no interest in being the next Marley Marl or Hurby Luv Bug. He was on some next level shit. He wanted to be a hip-hop businessman. In 1988, those kinds of statements were far-fetched. Being a hip-hop executive was high up the food chain. Def Jam and Uptown Records had only been in existence for a few years. There really was no precedent for Puff to follow, but he was not going to be deterred. His fearless persistence was his greatest asset. There *was* a time when it became my greatest headache.

"Playboy, can you do me a favor?" Puffy came through to check me just before break. He and his friends were going back to NY on one of the holiday breaks. His car was not going to be able to make the trip to New York and back. Puff needed me to rent a car for him. He knew I had good credit. *"No problem, I got you."* I rented a vehicle for him and he dropped me back on campus while he headed for his apartment in Maryland to get ready for the trip. The next day he called with bad news. *"Yo ha, I got something to tell you. I don't have good news, Playboy. My homeboy Walt G, yo he cold wrecked the joint and hit a tree". This nigga can't drive. He drove the shit into a damn ditch. I was like what the fuck. Now this cop, he is asking mad questions. You gotta come up here to help me straighten this shit up."*

Where I'm From: Growing Up Hip Hop

Puff hung up. I could not believe it. *Why was this nigga driving in the first place?* Puff came back to get me and now he was talking a mile a minute, trying to coach me on what I should say to the cop when we got there. *"Yo hah, you gotta tell this cop that you were the one that was driving"*. *"This nigga Walt G don't even have a license."*

I was livid. It took all the restraint I could muster not to lose it. I do not even know this dude and Puff wants me to lie for him. If I slipped up, I might be the one to go to jail. Puff is *still* in my ear. *"This is what you gotta say, you gotta lie boldface Playboy, you can't let him see that you nervous."*

I saw the car in the ditch and shook my head. Now the cop is asking *me* mad questions and making threats. *"You may end up with five points on your license. It all depends on how I feel tomorrow. If my wife doesn't give me no pussy tonight, then I'm taking it out on you. If I have a great night, I might just loosen up on you."* I could not believe what I was hearing. This shit could not get worse. I was wrong. I ended up with points on my license *and* the damages got added to my Amex card.

Every time I asked Puff for the money, he said he was broke. *"Yo man, I need my damn money! I gotta pay this bill, you know how this Amex shit is. This shit has gotta get paid on time! If you didn't have your no-driving ass man behind the wheel, this shit wouldn't have happened!"* I wasn't backing down. Neither was he. Our relationship was never the same.

The bill never got paid and my credit score dropped like the Dow Jones average. My shit was ruined for years. I was pissed at him for a very long time and he knew it.

Where I'm From: Growing Up Hip Hop

Track Thirteen
Two Kings in A Cipher

My experiences with Hurby saw me moving closer to my dream but I didn't wanna do it alone. I approached a fellow New Yorker on campus who seemed like he was serious, and we formed a rap group. My partner's name was Deric Angelettie and he was from Brooklyn.

Now it was time to make power moves. I went to the financial aid office and withdrew all my emergency funds and bought a boom box. My dorm room became our makeshift studio. Deric and I spent hours writing rhymes and making pause tapes. A pause tape is basically a primitive way of making beats without a whole lot of equipment. I would play and record my favorite part of a song. Then I would pause the tape deck at a certain spot, start the record over again until I had looped up enough to make a song.

A year later, I got my first royalty check. Herby paid me $7,500. I found a used car to buy for $5000, but Pops would not put me on his insurance. I had other options though. My good friend David McDonald talked me into buying a drum machine instead. We drove out to Wheaton, Maryland to Chuck Levin's Washington Music

Where I'm From: Growing Up Hip Hop

Center. It was where musicians in the local area got their equipment. I bought a brand new MPC 60 and a set of monitor speakers.

When my second royalty check came in six months later, I bought a Korg M1 keyboard and a Tascam four-track tape machine. Now I was rolling and could put together a quality album. I was the first one on campus with a drum machine and everyone wanted to see it. I spent every moment perfecting my music. The sound of my tracks spilled out into the hallway or out the open windows of my dorm room. Visitors constantly stopped by, but I didn't mind the traffic.

When I wasn't working on the album, I held down a gig at the JW Marriott hotel on Pennsylvania Avenue. I worked evenings as a bellman. The Marriot was a luxury hotel where so many of my customers were celebrities. It was not out of the ordinary to see people like James Brown, Jimmy Jam and Anita Baker checking in. Walter Cronkite, Rosie Grier and Dick Gregory were there too. I would meet them at the hotel entrance and carry their luggage to their rooms.

Although I was a student holding down a nine-to-five, rap was still in my blood. In between running bags, I wrote rhymes in my spare time. My manager Herb did not stress me. He was a cool brother from The Bronx who was supportive of my goals to get in the rap game. Things were moving quickly, especially when word got around that I made beats. It set off a series of power moves instigated by Howard University people.

Where I'm From: Growing Up Hip Hop

My classmate Ron DeBerry introduced me to Howard alumni Haqq Islam, vice president of A&R at Philadelphia International Records. I knew the label well. They produced many of the jams we rocked at Bootyland back in the day. When Haqq showed up to my dorm with Ron, I played my demo for him and he offered me a management contract on the spot. He was ready to get things moving. The next thing we knew, Deric and I were off to Philly.

My manager Herb hooked me up with some days off so I could travel. I would need them because we would have to go back and forth between DC and Philly to work on the album. My friend Ski-ter would drive us out there every other weekend. We slept on the floor of Haqq's apartment during the entire recording session. Our creative lens expanded.

We went from making tracks in my dorm to working at Kenny Gamble and Leon Huff's studio that produced classic records by legendary Philadelphia acts like The O'Jays, Teddy Pendergrass, Harold Melvin and the Blue Notes. Our days at Studio 309 was like going to school. Mr. Gamble dropped many jewels on us about the history of the business. He would also come to our sessions and give us pointers on our sound and mixes. We tried to leverage our connection with Gamble and Huff to secure a label deal. It was not easy. Most of them turned us down. A lot of it had to do with the market becoming oversaturated with Afrocentric groups like Brand Nubian, Tribe Called Quest and Public Enemy.

Where I'm From: Growing Up Hip Hop

West Coast rap music was becoming popular. It was a more aggressive style from what we were doing. It was also more appealing to a wider audience. It was spreading like a virus across the country and instead of running from it, record labels embraced it. They were on the lookout for any NWA or Ice Cube knock off they could find. We did not rap about guns or drugs. We did not rock jheri curls and skull caps. We were just about beats and rhymes. We rocked regular gear but there was one thing that made us stand out. The name of our group, Two Kings in A Cipher was more than just a name. It was a statement inspired by our exposure to Islamic teachings back in New York as well as our growing consciousness as black men.

I took it a step further. I was walking down the street in Georgetown when I looked in the window and saw a burgundy fez. I bought that joint right then. I was studying Tony Browder, Yosef Ben Jochannan, Ivan Sertima, and other great scholars of African history and growing spiritually every day.

I didn't see the fez as a prop or part of a costume for a video shoot or album cover. It was a symbol of power, authority, knowledge, wisdom, and understanding. According to my Moorish Science studies, the fez represented the seen and unseen. From the inside of my new crown, I saw a circle of 360 degrees---a *cipher* unseen by the naked eye. From the outside I saw two circles. One circle was the fez's opening that I placed on my head. The other circle that was seen only from a distance represented the manifest. They both were opposite ends of the spiritual and physical spectrum. One reflected who I was and the other who I was aspiring to be. From the moment I put it on, I was injected by a sense of purpose that fueled my creativity.

Biblical scriptures stated that the Word was made flesh. The Gods and Earths proclaimed let knowledge be born. Rakim constructed his God-Body pyramid brick by brick and it came out in his lyrics: *Self-esteem makes me super, superb and supreme."* My spiritual travels encompassed it all.

As I passed through the turnstile of self-definition, I shed my old names like a second skin. First, I was Ronnie Tuff, the young emcee who lived to rock the mic with my crew. Then I became Ron Juan, the debonair fly emcee steeped in a solid hip hop pedigree. Now I was *Amen-Ra*. I wore the name proudly like a precious jewel or amulet. I promised myself to never forsake it. In return, it gave me the buoyancy I would need to survive the treacherous waters of the record industry.

Haqq really believed in us. He saw our potential when a lot of people didn't. He had a vision to do big things with us. He was also Muslim, so he had the strength of the Nation of Islam behind him. There was one thing wrong---Haqq was power hungry and was always seeking to gain an edge. He devoured books like Sun Tzu's *The Art of War* and Machiavelli's *The Prince*. He also had a habit of quoting all the lines from *The Godfather*.

Like Don Corleone, Haqq would make us an offer we could not refuse. I remember it like it was yesterday. It was early '90 and we had just signed our management contract. Deric and I were in my dorm room working on new album material when Haqq showed up, contract in hand. *"Sign this. If you don't, you won't be able to work at 309 anymore."* We weren't sure what was going on. Being new to the game and not understanding the business side of things, we signed away all our publishing rights to Haqq. Gamble and Huff ended up passing on us, choosing to focus on managing their publishing catalog.

Bahia Records took a chance on us. They had a distribution deal with RCA, a major label with a long history going back to the fifties. Deric and I got a $2500 advance. We were given a recording budget and left Philly for Silver Spring, Maryland to begin work.

Although we were happy to be living our dream, clouds of conflict and discontent threatened to rain on our parade. Bahia label head Greg Peck signed us but whenever we were around him, he gave off a vibe that he did not like us. Greg was a Sunni Muslim like Gamble. I assessed that we got our deal on the strength of their spiritual brotherhood and our affiliation with Gamble. Greg had a couple of R&B groups that he gave more attention to and he would never let us forget that we were much lower on his radar of label priorities.

Where I'm From: Growing Up Hip Hop

RCA was not much better. At every meeting we had, we fought with Miller London and Skip Miller over everything. These guys were executives in charge of RCA's Black music department. They were from the old Motown days where they handled acts like The Commodores and Rick James. They hated rap music. Skip---who has since passed away---has been celebrated for breathing fresh air into RCA's urban music roster by signing young acts like SWV and working with the stable of rappers signed to RCA affiliate Jive Records.

These were days when the old guard where Black music's gatekeepers. Younger executives had not yet bum-rushed R&B and hip hop's show business ranks so we had to fend for ourselves and figure out how to make bricks without straw. Everyone told us that RCA was a graveyard for Black music. People predicted we would suffer, and they were right.

Bahia released our first single *Movin On 'Em*. We finished our *From Pyramids to Projects* album and started a promotional tour across the country. The label paid for our transportation and rented equipment for us.

Our first TV promotional spot was a disaster. When I found out I was going to be on TV, I was shook. I will never forget that day. We showed up for an episode of *Krush Rap*, a local hip-hop show broadcast in the Philly and DC areas. Mike Elliot was the host. When he started asking questions, our nerves got the best of us. I was a wreck. My heart was racing, and I could not get my words together. In the middle of the interview, I did the unthinkable and asked if we could stop for a minute. *"Can we cut here?"* Mike kept going. *"No, we can't cut here, the tape is rolling."* I was so embarrassed. It was worse when the show finally aired. The whole segment was all on tape. I trying to bail out of an interview on live TV, Deric was playing with his jacket zipper and Tone Fresh was looking away from the camera. I made up my mind that I would never play myself on TV again. I faced my fear of public speaking the way I conquered my fear of performing in crowds---head on.

The more I thought about the situation, I realized I was afraid of how people would view me. Most of the time my anxiety was in my head. I purged myself of my fear of rejection and criticism. Whenever I faced an audience for a performance, panel or speech, I wanted to make sure I was prepared I borrowed a strategy Winston Churchill used when facing down crowds. *Look at the people as if they weren't wearing any clothes. Let them be the laughing stock.* It worked and my confidence increased with every public speaking encounter. We hit every state, signed autographs, and performed at almost any place that would book us.

Our first stop was Atlanta to perform at Jack the Rapper, an industry networking convention for Black record, radio and retail people to observe the competition and check out new acts. We performed and got to meet a lot of industry cats. Atlanta was fun. It was the first time I had ever been to a strip club and experienced Southern hip hop up close and personal. As we passed through these Southern Bible Belt areas, we were shocked to find that most of the mom and pop stores weren't even carrying our CDs and tapes. Some only had one or two items in stock. Promotional posters were in the window but there was no product to sell to the people who stood on line all day to see us.

The upside was that every place we hit, there were groupies who were always willing to hook up. If we were not in stores, we would drive through neighborhoods and hit the streets, handing out pictures and signing autographs. We went to high schools and colleges to perform and do radio interviews. After a while I got sick of the same routine. There was a big difference between rocking mics at parties and shows and the promotional grind we were subjected to. I was starting to realize I enjoyed making the records more.

New York City was our last stop. It was good to be home. We checked into a Midtown hotel on 57th Street. Our gear was in the trunk. We were in the hotel less than a half hour when we went out to the car and found that someone made off with $3000 worth of equipment including the cordless mics we needed to perform with. I always heard how other groups were excited to wrap up their tour at Madison Square Garden or Nassau Coliseum. *So much for a triumphant homecoming.* This latest incident made me hate the road even more.

Where I'm From: Growing Up Hip Hop

My brother Derickson had begun to study a little bit of law and understood contract agreements. He looked over our management contract and found a loophole. Haqq had us signed to his management *and* production company at the same time. It was a conflict of interest.

When we stepped to Haqq and brought it to his attention, he knew that we had his back against the wall. I told him that we were not going to leave but he had to sign our publishing back over to us or else we would break the deal.

We ended up losing the RCA deal in the middle of working on our second album. Meanwhile Bahia Entertainment was dropped from RCA Records, which left us without a record deal. Haqq didn't slow down for long. He found a new group called Legacy who needed help with their demo, so he hired me to work with the group.

Legacy reminded me a lot of Jodeci, the R&B group who they idolized. If you closed your eyes and heard them sing, you couldn't tell the difference. They had a lead singer who could really sing. He was a little guy with a huge voice. We worked on a song together that helped them get a deal with Island Records, but my song never made the album deal.

After Legacy changed their name to Dru Hill they went on to have huge success. My experiences with the label and life on the road soured me on becoming an artist. When I heard rappers like Rakim killing it in the industry, I knew I couldn't compete. If I couldn't be an emcee, I would have to focus on *making* music for emcees.

Where I'm From: Growing Up Hip Hop

Where I'm From: Growing Up Hip Hop

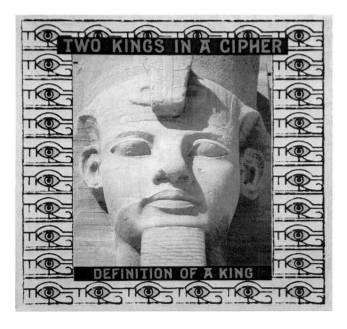

Two Kings In A Cipher

Glossary of Definitions

Amen-Ra — Amen is the infinite source of the life force and spiritual matter. Also known as the Hidden One or The Unseen Force. Ra is the rising sun.

D.O.P. — (Symbolic to Amen-Ra) Stands for "Deliverer Of Prophecy." It is the energy that delivers light (spiritual information) through music and lyrics to the pupils of the eyes or the pupils which are people. Also known as the Microphone Assassin.

King — (Master) One who knows, understands and controls all nature, motion, time and space.

Fez — (The hat worn by Amen-Ra) Named after one of the four capital cities of Morocco (a country in Africa). Known as the crowning of the head and represents knowledge.

Kemit — The original name for Egypt, meaning the Black land. It is also known as the cradle of civilization.

Egyptology — The study of Kemit and the development of the original man.

Melanin — Comes from the Greek word melanos, meaning Black. It is the most important molecule in the human body which screens out ultraviolet light from the sun. Melanin connects humans to the creative forces of the universe and makes them more in tune with nature.

Ka — The spirit that enters a person's life at birth and stays with him or her after death.

Pineal Gland — (Third Eye) An organ located in the interior of the brain at the exact midline of the forehead. It represents vision, insight and intelligence.

Cipher — A 360 degree circle which represents everything in life (person, place or thing). It is a completion of a cycle and also symbolizes the spirit.

3161-4-R

Tmk(s) ® Registered • Marca(s) Registrada(s) General Electric, USA. BMG logo ® BMG Music Bahia Entertainment logo™ Bahia Entertainment © 1991 Bahia Entertainment

Where I'm From: Growing Up Hip Hop

Where I'm From: Growing Up Hip Hop

TWO KINGS IN A CIPHER

SIDE III

Hitmen (1993-2003)

Where I'm From: Growing Up Hip Hop

Track Fourteen
<u>Still Paying Dues</u>

Hip hop was changing at the speed of light. Hyper James Brown or Sly Stone soul samples were over. Jazzy textured sounds by guys like DJ Premier and Pete Rock bounced across the five boroughs like a strong roaming signal. Intent on staying afloat, I changed right along with it. As soon as I hung up the mic for good, producer gigs materialized out of nowhere.

I landed my first job through an old Howard connection. Puff's longtime man Ward Corbett was working in A&R, securing producers to work with A.D.O.R., an up and coming rapper he and Puff knew from Mount Vernon now signed to Atlantic Records. A.D.O.R. had a high-pitched delivery and I knew exactly the kind of music that was perfect for his voice. I synched up the basslines from Quincy Jones' *Body Heat* and dropped in a Lords of The Underground vocal loop to create an ill track that was perfect for A.D.O.R.'s on-beat flow. He called it *Life Flow*. It wasn't a single. Just an album track. It didn't matter, I was on my way.

Where I'm From: Growing Up Hip Hop

Two years later, when the same *Body Heat* sample showed up on Tupac's number-one hit *How Do U Want It,* it was confirmation that I had a great producer's ear and could pick great records for beats.

It wasn't the first time. A year earlier in 1993, I was listening to the radio when I heard a DMC vocal that I used for an old 2 Kings and A Ciphers record back in '91. *"Down with the kiiiing. They wanna be down with the kiiiing."* Yo----when I heard that shit---I was euphoric! You would have thought I produced the joint! *My sample was the hook for Run-DMC's comeback single!* I wasn't pissed or bitter. I didn't hate. The song was better than ours. The *From Pyramids to Projects* album might have been far from a hit, but it felt good to know that *someone* was listening.

To keep myself in the public eye, I headed out to Atlanta for the Jack the Rapper industry conference. I ran into Kool Moe Dee while I was there. It was great to see one of my heroes in person. He had been in the game for about fifteen years by then and was still hungry. I handed him my demo tape and phone number. When I got home, I received a call from Moe.

He landed a situation with an independent label and wanted to use one of my tracks. *"I can pay $500. Where can I send you the contact.?"* I didn't budge. I needed at least fifteen hundred. *"That's not gonna work. My attorney fees are a thousand alone. If you can't match it then I'll have to pass on the project."* If I took short money, I would have to pay for a lawyer to negotiate the deal and I was not trying to do that. I was very excited and wanted to work with Moe D but in the end, I had to pass on the deal.

Six months later, I got a phone call from my man Genard. He was the one who introduced me to Moe. He had heard Moe's new Treacherous Three album *Old School Flava*. There was a track on the album called *Moe Money Moe* that sounded familiar. *"Yo Ron! I thought you didn't give the track to Moe Dee! It's on his group's album!"* When I got off the phone I went out and bought the album.

To say I was disappointed was an understatement. Moe D jacked at least two of my tracks from off the cassette I gave him and put them on his album. Instead of the original Miles Davis horn on the chorus, the Treacherous Three sang the hook rather than try to clear the sample. I let them live instead of suing. It was not worth it anyway. The album was a flop.

I had a good relationship with the Awesome Two going back to my Latin Quarter and emcee days. I did them a solid by featuring their group Ed O.G. and the Bulldogs in a limo scene of our *Movin on 'Em video*. I ran into Ed and his crew and gave them a few tracks off mine to check out. One of them would be the lead song on their *Going Outside My Head* maxi-single. Another rapper, Positive K purchased the original track that Moe jacked and released it independently as a record called *It's All Gravy*. These songs weren't hits, but it helped me get my weight up. I was constructing my musical resume, one joint at a time.

Where I'm From: Growing Up Hip Hop

Where I'm From: Growing Up Hip Hop

Track Fifteen
<u>Mistaken Identity</u>

The practicality and common sense I inherited from my Moms and Pops paid off. I had the foresight to keep my job at the Marriott. I made more money carrying bags than rhyming, anyway. I was able to get a nice one-bedroom apartment up on 12th and N in the Logan Circle area.

The neighborhood was a few years away from gentrification and was a haven for drugs and prostitution. I may have lived in a brand-new building, but when I stepped outside, I was back on 42nd Street all over again. In the daytime, the city was an attractive face of opportunity that was alluring. At night, the makeup came off and blemishes were everywhere. Pimps in jheri curls were holding down the block. Prostitutes were permanent fixtures. The sound of gunshots and sirens were the soundtrack of the city's underside.

Every morning when I left for work, I would have to fend off lusty propositions to dance with the devil. I always turned them down.

Where I'm From: Growing Up Hip Hop

Like thirsty brothers in the club clocking every move of a curvy stunner, these ladies knew my schedule. On cold nights, my spot could offer them a temporary respite from their nighttime solicitations. If they could entice me, they could seek shelter from the elements and make a dollar at the same time.

The light from my window was my cue to start my day. For my nocturnal neighbors, it was lights, camera, action. Time to hit their marks and get into character. It was nothing for me to walk out the door and find a prostitute in my face, greeting me with a seductive leer. *"Hey shorty, let's go inside. I'll make it worth your while. I'll make you smile."* I started putting on headphones to block them out. If they knew how much money I had on me, I could only imagine how hard they would press me. Every day I was coming home with five hundred dollars just in tips. I would never have to cash my weekly check.

It was the end of the month. Time to pay my bills and deposit some cash in the bank. I stuffed my pocket with singles, threw on a burgundy sweater and headed down to the post office. As I walked to the side counter to fill out some mail slips, I felt a hand touch my right shoulder from the back. I started to tense up when my martial arts training locked in.

I was thinking that maybe a basehead or stickup kid had followed me inside, trying to vic me. I planned my attack. *Bear weight on the balls of my feet. Move with the force of the attacker's grip.*

Keep the potentialities of my left striking side a secret. When he spins me around, take the pen in my left hand and go for his throat.

The jagged edge of an undercover cop's raspy voice released me from my defensive calm before the storm. *"Don't move, you're under arrest."* Everyone in the post office stopped what they were doing and turned toward me. The cop grabbed my hands from behind and put me in tight handcuffs. Their vise-like grip cut off my circulation. Three others appeared on cue. I thought they were customers, but they were there for backup.

They walked me to the back room of the post office and sat me down. While one interrogated me, one lady copped reached into my pocket and grabbed my stack of singles then threw it on the table. *"We got him."* I realized they thought I had robbed somebody. *"So, you think you were gonna rob the post office, huh?"* I was confused about the entire situation but remained calm.

A black cop jumped in the mix. *"Why are you carrying a stack of singles?"* I made sure my response was direct and respectful. I told them I worked for the Marriott as a bellman and I was going to the bank to deposit my earnings. The three cops were not buying it. They tried to tie me to a postal robbery over on 20th Street. They said I got away and then headed to this location to rob them. They were sure it was me but could not figure out why I was so calm and polite. They walked me into the back of a car and drove me to the location of the robbery.

Now I was in another dark back room in handcuffs. I felt like I was on trial for a crime I did not commit. My heart was racing a million miles a minute. I could not see anyone. I only heard the voices of a faceless jury haggling over a verdict that threatened to change my life forever. *"Is this him? the robber had a burgundy shirt too."*

Thankfully a voice of reason brought their deliberation to an abrupt end. *"It was a camouflage burgundy hoodie."* As the cops walked me back, one of them apologized and said how much of a well-mannered person I was.

I felt like spitting in his face, but I kept my cool. I knew when black people had run-ins with the law, they would try to argue their way out of the situation rather than staying calm and polite. If I had mouthed off at them, the outcome might have been different. They asked me where they could drop me off. I had them take me back to the same post office that they arrested me from. They dropped me at the front entrance. As I walked through the door, the postal workers were in shock. An hour ago, I was being led out in handcuffs. Now I was back. I walked up to the counter as if nothing happened, envelopes in hand. I greeted the clerk politely and continued my transaction. *"Can I have a book of stamps please?"*

Where I'm From: Growing Up Hip Hop

Track Sixteen
Grinding in Cali

When another producer gig came my way, my manager Herb looked out. He gave me a leave of absence after I received an opportunity from a Howard guy, Darnell Van Rensalier. Darnell reached out with an offer to move to LA to work on a project with his groupmates from Shai. After blowing up with their debut *If Ever I Fall in Love,* they were getting ready to record their next project.

Darnell liked my beats, and I had a little money saved so I figured it was a good look. I packed up my equipment, two pairs of jeans, three shirts and a few other things. I was only focused on building my equipment and record collection, I rarely bought new clothes. Anything that was outdated, I left behind. Darnell picked me up from the airport and drove out to Baldwin Hills where the guys were renting a house on Don Analis Place in a cul-de-sac in the center of the block.

When we pulled up to the house, I recognized it immediately. It was the same house where Ice Cube shot the video for *It Was A*

Good Day. He was renting it out to the group. Darnell and I got cool. Back then, I looked at Cali just like any jaded New Yorker. It did not have the energy I was used to. When the guys took me around, I was shocked to see palm trees *everywhere.* They added an exotic air to Cali's upscale areas. The trees did little to enhance the less affluent and run-down areas. Paradise never looked so scary.

The circle of young Black entertainers and famous people living in Cali was tight. You always ran into someone you knew. While hanging out, the guys bumped into Arnelle, an old acquaintance from Howard. She lived in Brentwood, a ritzy part of LA. Her father was a big shot around town. Arnelle invited us to a pool party she was having. She gave us the address: 380 North Rockingham Drive.

The guys were familiar with the area and found it with no problem. We pulled up to the house after being buzzed in at the gate. It was surrounded by elaborate landscaping that offered a lot of privacy. The house was modest yet lavish at the same time. When we got to the pool, girls were everywhere. There was a youngish-looking white cat hanging around while Arnelle's pops chilled in the house. We had a great time.

A few days later, I was chilling watching TV and saw a newsflash of a police car chase in progress. It was on every channel. When they cut back to pictures of a mansion, I nearly fell out of my seat. I turned the volume up. *I was just there.* All I heard was

Where I'm From: Growing Up Hip Hop

Rockingham and *murder*. When the pictures of the murder victims flashed across the screen, I recognized the guy's face. It was surreal. I felt like I had just barely missed the Manson murders. The sight of that white Bronco speeding down the expressway and a bizarre image of OJ Simpson in cuffs stayed with me for weeks.

I did two songs for Shai and when I turned them in, they demanded a five-way publishing and writer's split. This meant they were entitled to a share of the music I had worked on. Their last album sold three million copies and their leader Carl Martin wrote their biggest hit. It sold two million copies. He co-wrote another single that went gold, so he was getting major paper while the rest of the group were out in the cold.

I was not too comfortable though with splitting the pie five ways. I deserved more as a producer. Since I needed to get my foot in the door, I was willing to work things out. but I informed Carl that he would have to give me production credit on the songs I worked on. He agreed and we got to work.

While I was working in LA, D was shopping my tracks in New York and one of my tapes landed in the hands of my old Howard classmate Frantz Severe. He was working at Czar Entertainment, an up-and-coming East Coast-based company. They were working with Salt N Pepa, who were up to five million in sales of their latest album, *Very Necessary*.

Where I'm From: Growing Up Hip Hop

The company was run by Jimmy Rosemond. He was a street cat who called himself Jimmy Henchman. Just like Hurby, he was a Haitian cat who was making major moves in the industry. When he heard the tapes, he flew me out for a meeting. We spent the day together riding around the city of Manhattan as he made deals on his cell phone. As we vibed and got to know each other, Jimmy offered me and D-Dot a management contract. To show good faith, he placed a song for us before we signed the deal. That song, *What's Up Star* ended up on being on Def Jam's *The Show* soundtrack.

The artist slated to record the song was a female rapper from my old Queens days. She called herself Suga these days, but I knew her by her old emcee name Sweet-T. Sugar was signed to JMJ Records, a label owned by Jam Master Jay. Run-DMC's legendary DJ was now making moves behind the scenes.

After Suga recorded the track, Jimmy flew me out from LA a few weeks later for a mixing session with Jay. As we mixed the record, Jay gave me a few pointers on how to pull the bass out of the song. Jay was a legend, but he did not carry himself like one. He was cool. It was surreal to be working with one of my heroes who I grew up listening to. My stock was rising.

What's Up Star ended up being the second single on the album. Although things did not work out with Jimmy for various reasons, I appreciated the lookout. It felt dope to see my name on the credits of a major hip hop album.

Where I'm From: Growing Up Hip Hop

Unfortunately, things were not going so hot with my other project out in LA. When Shai's *Blackface* album dropped in May of '95, I raced to the record shop to cop a CD. I scanned the song credits for my songs *Let's Go Back* and *95*. My name was nowhere in sight. I was livid. I hit Deric over the phone. *"I can't believe these niggas, man. I didn't come all the way out for this, shit.* D calmed me down. He suggested I come back to New York. *"Here is where you need to be"* Deric had already moved back a year earlier. We continued our partnership. While I worked in Cali, I would send D-Dot my beats and he would shop them. By this time, I was staying with Darnell and his girl. I tried to make moves on my own, but it got to be too just too much. Unlike New York, LA was not big on public transportation.

Where I was from, *everyone* took public transportation. Here, only the have-nots rode the bus. I was only fifteen minutes from Sunset Boulevard by car, but by bus it took an hour and a half. I hated it. I would have to walk to a bus stop, wait an hour for the first bus. After it dropped me off at one location, I would then have to transfer to another bus which could take half an hour. The buses were always filthy.

All that walking caused me to lose mad weight and all the while I was thinking**,** *I didn't come out here to get in shape. I was here for the money.* I could not take another day of the sweat, filth and empty prospects. I made my mind up. It was time to go. I spoke to Darnell and he was cool about it. I was out. It was time to jump back in the water. I had no intentions on drowning. Staying afloat was my main objective and once again it was family who ended up tossing me a lifejacket.

I called Derickson in Mount Vernon. He had just purchased a new six-bedroom home. When he told me that I could stay with him, I put my equipment and records on an Amtrak train, and I flew back to New York.

Where I'm From: Growing Up Hip Hop

Track Seventeen
Everyday I'm Hustling

A few days after getting settled, it was back to work. The agreement I made with Derickson was that if he took me in, I would help with his political campaign. Crashing with-him for free meant I had to wake up super early to pass out flyers to early morning commuters headed for the city.

Derickson was running against incumbent mayor Ernie Davis who had Mount Vernon on lock for years. He had a reputation for being involved in corrupt situations. The thing that stood out most was that he and Derickson lived just three doors away from each other. At that time, I hated politics and could care less about what was going on. I just wanted to finish the job and get back to making beats.

When I was not working with my brother, my routine was crazy. Every day, I would walk about a mile to the train station and head into the city for meetings. If there were industry parties, I would hang out until midnight with just enough time to make it to Grand Central Station to catch the last train for Mount Vernon. At home, I camped out in my bedroom working on music. I would then take catnaps during the day, take a few calls and grab something to eat before hitting the drum machine. It was about the grind. It was either sink or swim and I was determined not to drown.

Things got a little easier when Pops passed down the LeBaron to me. He was not driving anymore because his legs were bad due to poor circulation. The wear and tear of New York City driving had taken its toll. The car had seen better days. A couple of hubcaps were missing. The leather interior was worn and sagging. I didn't care. It might have been a hooptie to the naked eye, but in my mind Pops' old car was a brand-new Acura.

I was grateful for the wheels. Now I could move around more easily. Derickson ended up losing his bid for mayor and it was a relief. Now I did not have to run all over Mount Vernon with him anymore. I could focus more on music. I had a 10k cushion saved from my old production jobs. I could buy my own food and gas. I would even kick up two or three hundred a month to my brother for rent.

Deric was still hustling my tracks and we landed a song on rapper Big Noyd's album. After we recorded it, Noyd got locked up. Out of the blue, Deric and I got a call from Kedar Massenburg. We knew each other from back in the old 2 Kings in A Cipher days when Kedar was rolling with our ex-manager. Kedar was on the come up. In between negotiating contracts for recording artists, he started up an entertainment company. One of his clients, D'Angelo was about to blow up. Always the go-getter and visionary, Kedar had a title for D'

Where I'm From: Growing Up Hip Hop

Angelo's music: *neo-soul*. He heard my tracks and played them for Rakim. He and Eric broke up a few years back and now he was gearing up for a solo run.

We set up a session at Soundtrack Studios on Broadway. When we hooked up in the studio, Ra's eyes lit up. *"Yo, Gee, I see you doing your thing, yah'mean? I'm feeling those tracks, son."* As always Ra was rolling with his crew. He had Bill Blass and Killer Ben with him. They were livewire dudes who had been down with Ra since his *Paid in Full* days. I remember Ben from hanging in the Latin Quarter. Guys like him were so thorough that nobody would try and test them because they would bust their guns at any moment.

Ra realized he knew me from hanging around back then. We got to talking about beats. He told me that he did most of the beats on his old albums. I was blown away by the fact that then greatest emcee of all time was as great beatmaker.

We knocked out two verses and a hook. Ra was still in top form. We scheduled another day to finish the song. I arrived early at Soundtrack Studios to add finishing touches and a mixdown. I waited patiently for Ra. At one in the morning, he finally calls. *"Yo Gee! the beat is pumpin? The bass is laid? Aaaight Gee, be there in a minute".* Three A.M. rolls around. No Rakim. I doze off after a while. I was still on the clock and getting paid, so it was nothing for me to wait. I woke up at five in the morning. *Now I know Ra ain't showing up*. We wouldn't work together for years.

It turned out that the car Deric was driving out to Mount Vernon from Brooklyn was the *same* black Chrysler LeBaron that I was driving (go figure). Deric would bring records to the crib. He had great ideas and we got to work.

One day Deric told me that Puff was putting a team of producers together and asked if I wanted to be down. *"Bad Boy's on fire. This is the move"* As Deric sang their praises, I didn't hesitate one second. *"Hell yeah!"* I replied, ready to get to work. Puff had come a long way from the days when I was introducing him to movers and shakers at Bayside Studios back in '88. His rise was quick.

During the years I was trying to stay afloat, Puffy had gone from being a background dancer in music videos to becoming an intern at Uptown Records where he did everything from carrying producer Teddy Riley's keyboards to grinding for label exec Andre Harrell. From there, he graduated to head of A&R where he was instrumental in launching the careers of Father MC, Mary J. Blige and Jodeci.

Now he was head of his own label with a roster of acts. He was also a producer in his own right. Bad Boy was just beginning its run of R&B and hip-hop hits. Rappers Craig Mack and The Notorious BIG had *huge* records out that put the East Coast back on top in terms of rap music.

Where I'm From: Growing Up Hip Hop

I remembered Biggie from my LA days. I was at a music conference with Shai when I saw Biggie chilling with his entourage in the parking lot. My track that Moe Dee jacked had gotten around to Biggie's people. His Junior Mafia crew ended up doing a demo to the track. I introduced myself and thanked him and kept it moving. Puff was doing very good. He was not pushing his Volkswagen Cabriolet anymore. He had moved up to a 325 Beemer. He had finally arrived.

Up to this time, he relied on outside producers like Easy Mo Bee, Pete Rock and DJ Premier. Now he was ready for a change. When Deric told me that Puff wanted to put together a production team, for once I felt like I was in the right place at the right time. *This could be my shot.* When I showed up at Puff's studio, he didn't exactly welcome me with open arms. He greeted Deric warmly. He gave me a pound but was very distant. I was in his presence, but it felt more like I was on the outside looking in. After the rental car fiasco, we had not spoken in years. Our beef was still frozen in time. I could not figure out if he was mad at me or just did not want to give me the time of day. Our roles were reversed. Five years ago, I was the man with the connections. *I* was the one with the keys to a world Puff yearned to gain access to. Now *he* was the man.

I swallowed my pride and kept coming around. I did not just want to be down. I *needed* to be down. It was not easy. Every time I came through, Puff ignored me. When Puff finally put a contract together. Deric was reluctant to sign. *"Yo Ron, you good but me...I don't know."* Deric was an emcee at heart. He felt he wasn't ready to be a record producer. I understood but there was no way I was going to do this without my man. I still remember how I felt when the Super Lovers broke up and started making moves on their own. *"We need to go into this together. Listen, let's just do it like we always have. I make the beats and you shop 'em. We split the check and the credit like we been doin'."* We shook hands and just like that, Two Kings in A Cipher were on our way to becoming Bad Boy hitmen.

Where I'm From: Growing Up Hip Hop

Where I'm From: Growing Up Hip Hop

Introducing..

"THE HITMEN"
Wednesday, Dec. 11, 1996
Daddy's House Recording Studios
321 W. 44th St., NYC

Track Eighteen
<u>Bad Boy</u>

I am a laid-back dude. I was all about business. Let everyone else shine. Rakim said it best: *One thing I don't need is the spotlight, because I already got light.* I have to say that during Bad Boy's run, NOBODY did it like us. We were the phoenix rising out of the ashes of Black music's glorious past, forging the old and new. Our assembly line approach to making hits locking down radio and the charts was a throwback to the Motown hit factory of the 1960s.

In the 1970s, my mentors Gamble and Huff added classical string arrangements to their Philly Soul compositions. Critics called it "putting a bow-tie on the funk." At Bad Boy, we did the same thing. We gave hip hop music a more lush and bigger sound. The Notorious BIG was a charismatic artist. He had a huge presence. He had a powerful voice. His rhyme style was very aggressive and upfront. The music had to be grand. Dramatic. It had to make a statement.

Listen to joints like *Lean Back, Disco Inferno* and *If I Ruled the World (Imagine That)* and you will see the Bad Boy influence on those Fat Joe, 50 Cent and Nas records. Go back and check the music from Rick Ross and DJ Khaled too.

All those classic West Coast productions? Great records. Clean sound. One thing they were missing was Bad Boy's heavy bottom and hi-hats. You heard it on Dr. Dre's *Chronic 2001* album and records like Snoop's *Down for My Niggaz*. Music critics give DMX lots of credit for ending our run and restoring rap's grittiness, but X's BIGGEST records have traces of the Bad Boy formula. Joints like *Hypnotize*, *Been Around the World* and *All About the Benjamins* are the origin of it all. Back in the days typical rap anthems like *Hip Hop Hooray* were built around catchy hooks.

We *redefined* the rap anthem by making sure the *music* was as important as the hook. Unlike other R&B and rap producers whose production approach was more self-contained, our team worked on each other's tracks. This continuity strengthened our brand and set us apart from the rest. There might be six cats sharing writing credit, but we did not care. It was not just about looping up a familiar sample and expecting a hit to fall from the sky.

Bad Boy was a rap music exfoliate. We scrubbed away abrasive layers of underground hip hop productions and buffed it out to a healthy sheen. Before we came along, East Coast rap music was more insular. It was like cats were making records for each other instead of a larger audience.

Where I'm From: Growing Up Hip Hop

I loved it but I learned from Puff that the "for us by us" creativity would only work for so long. If producers wanted to make headphone music, that was cool. We wanted *radio*. Purists may have felt that we watered down the music just to get commercial airplay. They were wrong. Puff's kicked a rhyme on *Don't Stop* that sums our movement precisely. Our music's vibrant energy lifted your mood.

When DJs like Funkmaster Flex went into a Bad Boy set in clubs like the Tunnel, the crowd would always lose it. We had artists with unique voices and distinctive nuances in the tradition of singers like Teddy Pendergrass, Eddie Levert and Billy Paul. Jadakiss' voice had a raspy arrogance, Carl Thomas's smoky baritone was like Nat King Cole and Lil' Kim's husky cockiness gave her rhymes a deadly edge. Faith's gospel-honed vocals could either take you to church or to the club. She was versatile. She could sing background harmonies and then switch up to give you leads. Mase and Loon were laidback and cool. They always hit you with the ear candy.

Nobody rode beats like them. Their precise on-beat flows were like Michael Jackson's percussive way of singing on classic soul joints like *Show You the Way to Go*. These guys' voices were like drum kicks. They always stayed right in the pocket---their voices sunk into the parchment of R&B collaborations as if they were ink. Put on one of their records and I *dare* you not to sing along (or dance). Slim's tenor voice cut through an endless swath of R&B vocal groups so when you heard a 112 joint, you knew it was them.

Where I'm From: Growing Up Hip Hop

Some female singers are just a muse for their producers. They get lost in the tracks. Mary J. Blige's identity was solid like concrete. She ALWAYS held her own whether she rocked with the hottest producer or flyest rapper. Collaborators like Kelly Price sang dope hooks. She was so good that she parlayed her gifts into her own recording career. Mario Winans straddled the line between producer and artist. That's just a few of the bullets we had in the chamber.

The Notorious Big did *everything*. He was the complete package. He was a rapper but his classics *Juicy, Big Poppa* and *One More Chance* held their own against R&B records. They could be inserted into daytime radio playlists and not miss a beat. He was the Otis Redding to Bad Boy's Stax Records, our label's flagship artist.

Then there was the ringmaster of this revolving galaxy of stars. The straw that stirred the drink---Sean "Puffy" Combs, our formidable leader in all his regal pageantry. Otis Redding's fatal crash crippled Stax Records. Teddy's paralyzing car wreck reduced Philly International to a shell of its former self. We were different.

When Bad Boy went through similar challenges, Puff would insert himself into the lineup and take the label to the championship. He picked up the baton and carried it to the finish line. When did you ever see Berry Gordy come from behind his desk, grab a mike and make a record that goes 7x platinum *and* win a Grammy? Never! Like Def Jam records, Bad Boy was the product of a business relationship between the corporate record industry and the hip hop world.

Where I'm From: Growing Up Hip Hop

The same way Clive Davis formed a joint venture partnership with Gamble and Huff back in the 1970s, he linked up with Puff in the 1990s. Finally, Black music was on the grand stage where it belonged. R&B and hip hop had access to recording and video budgets traditionally reserved for white artists. We were a long way from the days when Michael Jackson was the only artist on MTV. Now our videos were in daily rotation across all formats. Our joints were like movies. They had celebrity cameos. They were expensive. *Really expensive.* No matter how lavish and extravagant we got, the music lived up to the hype. The bigger the visuals, the bigger the sound. In the middle of the joint, we would drop in a break from an old club record just because we could do it. It was as if our joints were film soundtracks. It used to be that the *concert* was an artist's ultimate attraction. No more. Bad Boy made the music video the main draw. One percent of our million-dollar budget is still more than the cost it takes to make an average video today. It will never happen again.

When Mariah Carey ditched her pop diva persona and rocked with Bad Boy, the industry lost its mind. How could the girl next door be with *those guys?* That formula we gave her? She is still following it today. She ended up doing what Janet and Whitney struggled to do---stay connected with the times by making contemporary music. Mariah's closing in on three decades in the game. Still working with hot and up-and-coming producers. It all started with a joint that Puff and Hitman Stevie J laced her with.

Where I'm From: Growing Up Hip Hop

Records like *All About the Benjamins* sounded like nothing on the radio. Bad Boy didn't just co-opt that jet-set lifestyle usually associated with rock stars; we took their music along for the ride. Sting's *Every Breath You Take* was already a catalog hit, but Bad Boy blew the joint up even further. If you messed with us in '97 you were guaranteed a hit.

When Elton John let Sting hear it for the first time, he told Sting four words: *You're gonna be loaded.* Bad Boy were thoroughbreds with the star power of the Showtime Lakers of the Eighties. We dominated the music game like the Bulls of the Nineties. We were like Golden State—an emerging dynasty with our sights set on platinum sales. During our championship run, a lot of artists were banished to the sidelines. You had to step your game up.

If you were an R&B ballad guy and wanted to hear your records in the club, you called us for that work. Wanted to leave that pop shit behind and go back to your R&B roots? You called us. Leaders became followers. Everybody jacked our formula. Labels. Producers. Classic artists who fell on hard times were able to turn things around thanks to the crazy sample clearance fees we paid out. If the song was a hit (it usually was), it was a windfall for them. The ones who were already rich? We made them richer.

The critics mistook us for hip hop cannibals gutting out funky breaks of old song catalogs. We respected the music. We added our own flavor. Our fingerprints were on everything.

Where I'm From: Growing Up Hip Hop

The musical landscape was like a crime scene and we were guilty as charged. You had to have that smooth record or remix with the chick on a hook. That tag-team chemistry of Puff and Mase was golden. One by one (I won't name names) the entire industry fell under the Bad Boy spell.

When the smoke cleared, out went the chew sticks, Carhartt gear and the hoodies. In came the Cartier and Versace glasses, silk shirts and linen outfits. Videos shifted from gloomy project backdrops to breezy white sand beaches and crazy conceptual imagery. You had to keep up.

Pre-Bad Boy, female rappers in the early nineties had that screw face posturing thing going on. All that screaming and shit. After we came along, they left it behind and gravitated back to being feminine and sexy.

Back in the days your *chain* was your symbol of success. I remember when Eric B was the only hip hop cat with a Rolls Royce. In the beginning you might have had a Pathfinder or a Benz 190 if you were doing it. Later it was a Range Rover. Now you had to go big or go home. That meant you had to be pushing wide-body Benzes with V-12 engines. Bentley Arnages, Azures, GTs and Continentals. Later it was Phantoms and Maybachs. All of that was inspired by Bad Boy. Our photo shoots were like motion picture stills. I remember one shot we had the whole team posing next to a helicopter and a fleet of luxury cars. We pissed a lotta people off. One group made a video to diss our movement. Guess what? *They're* in designer suits now.

When cats took shots at us, Deric bodied them like Rakim taking out all twenty-one emcees, but he didn't do it with rhymes. Deric created the Madd Rapper character, a parody of a washed-up underground rapper watching the Bad Boy parade go by---dismissive one moment and envious the next. He was a metaphor for all those rappers taking jabs at us. Big and Mase were infamous for taunting the critics. One of Mase's verses said it all: *all we hear is platinum that/platinum this/ platinum whips/nobody got no platinum hits."*

In the Eighties Slick Rick dismissed his rap adversaries as "crumbs." We called them *playa haters.* Worse than the backstabbers who smiled in your face and schemed to take your place, playa haters were quick with a negative comment and never gave you your props. Bad Boy turned that shit into a household word. Guys like the Funk Brothers, The Clan and The Corporation were behind Motown's greatest hits. MFSB was the engine that drove Philly Soul. These cats were talented but back in the day, individual credit and financial compensation eluded them. Today, it might take a year for producers to get paid. Up and coming producers might work with hot artists for free. They might have to give up rights in exchange for "exposure." At Bad Boy there was none of that. We were *well* compensated. We got advances for future work. Whenever we tracked a song, there was always a check waiting for us at the administration office.

Where I'm From: Growing Up Hip Hop

When Jay-Z, R. Kelly and anybody was somebody came through for beats, we always got half up front. Puff could have tied us into some long-term exclusive production deal, locking us up forever. He let us eat. We were free to get money outside of Bad Boy and become wealthy in the process.

Our ability to revive the joy and celebratory mood of the records from our youth was not a fluke. We didn't just catch elusive lightning in a bottle once. We did that shit multiple times. Let's go back for a minute. Before Bad Boy, rap music was an underground affair. Producers and artists went out of their way to not make anything that was evenly remotely close to commercial music. If you did, you were considered a sellout. I won't mention any names, but certain artists were heavily criticized or lost their careers when they stepped out the box. Artistic integrity meant only catering to your core audience and no one else.

As the sound became more gritty artists changed their styles to compete. It was about being hardcore. It was a soundtrack to a world where hip-hop artists seemed preoccupied with making music for each other and not for a wider audience. During an interview, Biggie told a story of how a rapper in Oakland wanted to battle him for a dime sack of weed. Biggie already had an ounce in his pocket. His thoughts on battling basically reflected the attitude of our artists:

"To me battlin' is some shit that you used to do when you ain't had shit. When you were trying to prove yourself. Niggas ain't had

shit back then. They ain't had nothin' to do but to gain that crown of being the nicest emcee. Now me? I'm tryin' to be the emcee with the most money. That's my shit now."

We loosened things up. Music became more polished. It had more live instrumentation. We combined the best of both worlds. We kept that underground ruggedness but gave it a sense of style and slickness. We were not the first. We were just an extension of what came before us.

The Sugar Hill guys used live instruments on early rap recordings. Teddy Riley mixed hip hop and R&B, creating the New Jack Swing vibe that preceded Uptown Records hip hop soul. We were next. We had respect for everything that came before us. Make no mistake, we loved hip hop. We just did it in a different way and it all went down in Midtown Manhattan at 321 West 44th Street.

Where I'm From: Growing Up Hip Hop

Track Nineteen
<u>Making Moves with Puff</u>

Daddy's House Recording studio was a hit factory. It was one thing being in the studio at 309 back in Philly but this was something else. Daddy's House was not just a studio. It was our home base. Bad Boy artists were there every day. If they were not writing their rhymes and working on songs, they were recording vocals almost every day of the week. The studio always stayed busy. Someone constructed the track's framework. Another would have sample ideas. Someone else would provide live instrumentation and create the overdubs.

Most of the sessions took place from mid-afternoon or early evening until the sun came up the next day. Studio sessions were booked around the clock. Whenever I showed up for work, it was like watching an open-air drug bazaar. Aspiring songwriters and producers gathered around the building like a cheese line, standing outside of the building looking to get put on. It was like wolves stalking their prey in the wilderness. They were dying to get inside the studio to see what was going on, but bodyguards and receptionists were always on hand to stop the bum rush. If you *were* able to pass a tape along to one of us or got a pass to get inside, you were lucky.

There was great camaraderie, but we always competed amongst ourselves to see which producer had the most cuts on an album. Whoever had that heat could always count on an artist in search of a hit to seek them out. Because we were a tight unit, we were able to craft a signature sound, no matter whose production it was. Our work ethic and consistency set us apart from other producers and we never had to worry about getting song placements from other artists. Now I knew what it was like at Philadelphia International when they made all those hits. We had a dope squad.

We had Younglord, the teenaged producer prodigy. He was nice on the production tip. He was signed to Puff at sixteen and was one of his first music guys. Younglord was very inquisitive and diligent. He was always looking to soak up knowledge and learn everything from equipment to music publishing. Chucky Thompson was another one who got with Puff early. He started out by submitting tracks to Puff and ended up producing a lot of early joints for Bad Boy before we all got together as a team. He had tremendous insight as a producer. Even though he was from DC, his creative lens extended beyond East Coast music. He was the man behind *Big Poppa,* the record that launched Biggie's mainstream popularity outside of New York. He also played an instrumental role in creating Mary's *My Life*. Chuck had a go-go background and played a variety of instruments. He had a good ear. He could hear a sampled track and replay it completely with all the instruments.

Stevie J. was probably the most musically inclined of all of us. He could play guitar, bass, drums and keyboards. He was dope on the MPC machines. He had been in the game for a while working with Jodeci. Nashiem and Chucky started out working together. He came up with loops and beats for Chucky to play over. Very soulful. Prestige was a dope producer and did some great records for the label. Jay-Dub was an ATL guy. He flew up to New York to work. He had a close bond with the artists.

Deric and I worked together as usual. Inside there were two mixing studios opposite of each other. One was the SSL room and the other was the Neve Room. This is where the engineers worked---guys like Prince Charles Alexander, Tony Maserati, Steve Dent, Lane Craven and Mike Patterson. The best in the game. The floor-to-ceiling speakers were so loud I would always have to bring air plugs to the sessions. Besides the rumbling bass, weed and cigarette smoke were always a constant, except when Puffy was around.

Whenever Puffy was in the building it was all business. He was focused. During recording sessions when word got out that Puffy was on his way to the studio, it was like the president was coming. Everyone scattered like roaches. The cigarettes and pungent weed aroma were replaced by the scent of air fresheners. I always made it my business to come to the studio during the week and keep all my music handy. We stored our tracks on floppy disks back then and I stayed ready. I would keep my car trunk full of disks in case one of my songs were chosen. There was no time to lose, because if Puffy liked a track, he would ask you to lay down a recording right away. If you weren't prepared, you would miss out on an opportunity. The great thing was, if your track was chosen, there would be a check waiting for you.

The administrative office might have been where the checks were going out, but the midi room in Daddy's House was the place where the cash was rolling in for Bad Boy. I couldn't get a good vibe working out of that room, so I created my beats at home. Puffy didn't like us making beats outside of the Midi room because it meant that he couldn't charge production time to an album budget if the beats were made elsewhere. Sometimes I would give him a tape with beats that I made in my home studio and he would lose it on purpose!

When I passed my cassettes over to Puff, he would never listen to them. One day I found one of my cassette tapes laying around the studio on one of the tables in Daddy House. I realized right then that I was not a priority for Puff. He was playing favorites when it came to picking producers and I was not on his list. Sometimes when I would see him, he would not acknowledge my presence. I started getting more aggressive. After a while I would walk up to him, shake his hand and hold my glance with an intent stare.

Where I'm From: Growing Up Hip Hop

If I was going to be a Hitman, I wanted to make sure that he knew I was there. Some nights I would wait around, in hopes of having a late meeting with him. When I finally got to sit with him after waiting for hours, it was the same scenario. He would scan the tape and listen for a few seconds. Then it was on to the next. The response was always the same. *"Sorry playboy, I ain't feeling it."* My beats had a very dark vibe back then and more suited for movie soundtracks.

Puff didn't care for my hardcore style. He was more interested in soulful sampled-based tracks like what Carlos Broady and Nasheim were doing. It was back to the drawing board. I switched up and started polishing up the music, switched it up again a bit and added some commercial polishing with soulful samples. As much as I tried to accommodate Puff, I felt he was sleeping on some bangers. He really was. On that tape was the genesis of future hot joints destined to become my signature hits. For now, it was just *next...next...next....* Bills were piling up that needed to be paid. I had just copped a new Honda Accord LX. It was time to get things moving. It felt like he just did not care. This went on for almost six months.

One day out of the blue, he apologized for playing me. He said he had a lot on his mind and was thinking about too many other things. He was under mad pressure. *Finally, an opening.* It still was not wide enough though for me to penetrate that Hitman circle.

Where I'm From: Growing Up Hip Hop

Track Twenty
<u>Trinidad</u>

Deric came to my house with a bunch of records for me to hear. *"Yo Ron—check this out."* He put on a Herb Alpert album and a familiar keyboard blast hit me dead in my face, taking me back to my childhood in Queens. I turned the music up and bass filled the room. Clearly, I was having a moment. As soon as I heard the breakdown, it was over. *"Dope, right?"* D-Dot broke me out of my trance, and we smiled at each other in mutual agreement. *Rise* passed my head-nod litmus test.

There was no way that we were not going to create a track that would bring this sample to life. As my production career was heating up, Moms and Pops' careers were winding down. They were retired and having the time of their lives. It had been nearly thirty years since they left Dominica for New York and now things were coming full circle. They would go back and visit often. They kept our old house on the island and rented out the top floor and stayed on the bottom.

Where I'm From: Growing Up Hip Hop

Pops was determined to retire there while Moms wanted to stay in the States where her kids were. Every February, Dominica celebrated its independence with a big festival complete with a large carnival. My parents never missed it. They flew down for the carnival like normal. A few days into the trip, Moms called with news that I did not expect to hear. *"Ronald, your father passed away today. He's gone."* I could not believe it.

I didn't know where Moms found the strength to call each one of her children and tell us the bad news. Like most West Indian parents, Pops was a no-nonsense cat. By the time I was born, he was much older. He was not the type to walk me to the store or throw a football with me. He was too busy working. It didn't matter, I learned more from him by just watching.

At that moment, I promised myself that I would have a family by the time I turned thirty-five. I wanted to be young enough to enjoy life and spend as much time as I could with my children. As Pops' life flashed before my eyes like a human highlight reel, everything he did seemed to take on more meaning. Leaving his beloved law enforcement job to come to New York to work those security and airport jobs. Abandoning a life of comfort to one where he worked all the time. Giving me his car as I was running around the city with no transportation of my own, coming through in the clutch when I needed it.

Where I'm From: Growing Up Hip Hop

He and Moms had created a nurturing family that were always there for me. They never made me feel bad for taking a non-traditional career route. Just as I was on the cusp of doing something great, Pops was gone. He was seventy-two. Even in death, Pops' prudence and practical foresight lingered. He was buried in his beloved homeland and his retiree benefits with American Airlines, allowed my entire family to fly down to Dominica to say goodbye one last time. Today, whenever I reflect on his life a quote I remember comes to mind: *His heritage to his children wasn't words or possessions, but an unspoken treasure, the treasure of his example as a man and a father.*

It was time to head back to New York. My heart was still heavy. I boarded the plane and put my head back in the seat reflecting on how far I had come.

Almost twenty-five years ago I was on a plane like this headed for New York to rejoin my family. Fifteen years ago, I was taking my first steps towards a career in hip hop. Ten years back, I embarked on what seemed like a never-ending journey of false starts and disappointments in this music game. Now I was living out my dream for real. That four-year old wide-eyed boy was on his way to becoming a big producer. A Bad Boy producer. I was not quite thirty and I sensed a great future was in front of me. I felt triumphant.

As I basked in the moment, my utopian spell was broken by an abrupt landing. I had touched down at JFK. As I walked out of the airport with my bags, I passed a ticket counter and briefly thought of

Where I'm From: Growing Up Hip Hop

Pops. A line from a Soul II Soul joint from back in the day was on repeat in my head. I mouthed the words softly like a Buddhist chant, trying to calm my nerves as the sound of taxi cab horns pierced my brain like needles. *Back to life, back to reality.*

When I got back, the deal was finalized. I signed a contract with Bad Boy Management. In exchange for paying a management fee, I secured the labels services to act on my behalf and steer future outside production gigs my way. For now, it was about Bad Boy. Puff was ready to get down to business. *"For the next two years, I wanna have radio on lock. Call the girlfriend, wifey, or whatever, and let 'em know that you're not gonna be around for a few weeks."*

It was winter 1995 and Puff was hungry. If other labels had the year Bad Boy had, they would be kicking back in celebration mode. Not Puff. He did not look back. He was looking ahead. It was hard to celebrate if he wanted to. A dark cloud of conflict lingered over Bad Boy. It affected our mood and no matter what we did, we just could not shake it. Last year, Tupac was robbed and shot at Quad Studios on his way to a session. In a *Vibe* magazine article, he laid the blame at Biggie, Puff and Andre's feet claiming he was set up.

When Biggie's *Who Shot Ya* hit the streets, conspiracy theories spread like wildfire. The joint was old. Biggie recorded it long before the shooting. The track first saw the light of day as an interlude on Mary's *411* album. Everyone had their opinions. The media fanned the flames. A line was drawn in the sand and just like that, two of the biggest industry markets were drawn into a civil war.

Big and Pac were two friends from opposite coasts who were the biggest stars in hip hop at that moment. It was a déjà vu moment. Michael Jackson and Prince all over again. Because they were not friends and never recorded together, the world lost an opportunity to witness the possibilities of their joint greatness. A decade later, two rap giants upped the ante. They had already done one song together, but it was not meant to be. Big and Pac's friendship would never recover.

Things were getting crazy by the minute. Puff needed a break. He was also negotiating a deal and did not want to get caught up. He was ready to make another power move and wanted no distractions. *"We're gonna get away from all this drama, put our heads together, and when we come back, we're coming back with hits."* Puff was plotting to conquer the airwaves. Me, Deric, Nasheim and Stevie J all sat quietly in the studio as Puff ran down his plan of action. *"The name of the album will be Goodfellas and you all will be my hitmen. Our goal is to take over New York City radio and I want to make sure that every single record that the DJs will play will be a Bad Boy Record."* As Puff solemnly explained this new strategy, I felt a chill up my spine.

It was like a scene from a Mafia movie. Puff had already booked time in Trinidad at Caribbean Sound Basin Studio. Caribbean

Sound was owned by Robert Maraval, an East Indian entrepreneur from a wealthy family who owned a host of businesses on the island.

When we got there, passing through customs with my equipment was a headache. The customs officials wanted to know why I had all this equipment and what I was going to do with it. I had to leave it at the customs office until Robert pulled some strings to have all my gear released to me. We were rolling deep. Besides me and Deric, Puff brought along Stevie J, Nashiem and Carlos Broady to assist with production. Faith and 112 were with us to provide vocals. To ensure our sounds were tight our engineers Axel, Tony and Doug also made the trip. Puff spared no expense in assembling his team of heavy hitters. The studio had a huge area with a twenty-four track SSL board with an additional production midi room. Bedrooms were on the top floor. There was a gym upstairs and a pool and basketball court out back. There was even a cafeteria.

Our routine was set. We would get up in the morning and hit the gym to get our juices flowing. Then we would work until five in the morning. By midnight though, my eyes were on fire and I struggled to stay awake. My body clock was still adjusted to my Marriot shift. I was also used to moving around instead of spending hours sitting at a machine.

Everyone would laugh because I couldn't hang until daylight. After a while, Puff created shifts for our guys while rotating Caribbean Sounds in-house engineers to make things easier.

We worked in teams of two. Deric and me. Nashiem hooked up with Carlos while Stevie and Puff worked together. When one group was in the midi room making beats, the other was at the SSL tracking their finished beats.

We completed at least sixty tracks. Puff rented huge stadium speakers to get the feel of what the songs would sound like in a club setting. Everyone had a hand in the creative process. When you looked at the credits, it could be up to ten names. No matter who produced the music, anyone who participated got a writer's credit.

This pioneering arrangement would become an industry standard. Faith and 112 were not only singers. They wrote too. 112 recorded their debut *Only You* and they collaborated with Faith on *I Just Can't,* a song Puff and Stevie produced. The track was built around the same jazz sample used in a song that was killing radio--- rapper Busta Rhymes' *Whoo Hah (Got You All in Check).* It was intended for R&B singer Aaliyah.

It seemed perfect for her. Faith even sang the lyrics in Aaliyah's breezy style. When she passed on the record, Faith used it for herself. It ended up being used for a movie soundtrack. Aaliyah and her mother came down to Trinidad with the rest of the crew. She was looking for songs for a new album she was recording.

During breaks we would talk and get to know each other. She shared with me that she was originally from Brooklyn but living in

Chicago. During our downtime sometimes we would hang out at the beach or hit the clubs. Aaliyah was only a couple years into her career. She was only about sixteen or seventeen but had an air of maturity beyond her years. Bad Boy was on fire and the fact that she passed on one of our tracks offered a glimpse of how adamant she was in shaping her career.

Aaliyah's intuition was dead-on. Her album *One in A Million* was a smash. Unlike other artists of the day jockeying for our tracks, Aaliyah had a vision for her own sound, and it worked. When she died five years later, it was a tragedy. It felt eerie. In '96 she was with us in Trinidad. After a video shoot in the Bahamas, her plane crashed killing everyone aboard. It would have been great to work with her. *Rest in peace, Aaliyah.*

During a session, Deric and I came up with a plan on how to utilize the *Rise* sample. I programmed a track I made into my MPC-60 and put the drums to go under the sample before I added analog bass sounds to give it a bottom. After I looped and programmed the record, I sampled kick and snares through the ASR10. It also had stock bongos and hi-hat sounds that fit the track nicely.

Once the track got to Puff, he flipped out. *"Yo...this shit right here is fire, playboy."* He could not stop playing it, and that's how I knew we had something. It was his favorite track and he wanted it for Biggie. All we needed were his vocals. We kept it in the family and got Pam Long from Total to do the hook. Being an island boy, I would venture out to sample West Indian delicacies like curry chicken and roti. It was like being home again. In between sessions we would head out to Horseshoe Beach. The vibe was so laid back we took everything in stride, even after we had a small fender bender on the winding hills leading to the beach.

    When Puff hopped on a flight back to attend the Soul Train Awards out in LA, I found time to slip away to Dominica. It was only an hour away and I looked forward to spending time alone to recharge my battery. We had plenty of ammunition. All we needed to do was load the bullets in the chamber and set our sights on our target. *Radio*.

Where I'm From: Growing Up Hip Hop

Track Twenty-One
The King of New York

I hadn't seen Biggie since I was out in LA, but that all changed after I signed my deal. *"Burgundy joint, right?"* Biggie raised his hand over his head. His deadpan humor was hilarious. I couldn't help but laugh. He was referring to the burgundy fez I wore during my TKO days. Every time we saw each other, that was how he greeted me. Jay Z stopped by Daddy's House to check on Biggie occasionally. When he did, I was lucky to have my camera with me. I took a lot of pictures but when I got home, I realized I hadn't spooled the film in the camera correctly. *Damn.* I still regret not catching those rare moments of Biggie and Jay in the studio.

    Biggie had a unique studio routine. He would plant a peanut butter jar of weed down in front of him, roll up and just vibe to the music. He didn't write anything down. He might talk a little, crack jokes or he would just sit back and chill. This could go on for thirty minutes or maybe a few hours. This caused Biggie to run up crazy studio bills. In a different situation he would have been another label's

financial nightmare. That was the genius of Puff. By having his own label and studio along with producers under contract, he could accommodate Biggie's creative idiosyncrasies. When he finally hit the booth, his verses were always on point. He could fit verses and cadences in tight pockets of beats. It was like Biggie was playing Pac-Man. His mic was a joystick, navigating his rhymes through a maze of twists and turns. Some cats just have dope rhymes but turn in mediocre vocal performances. Hip hop lyricism isn't always about having a complex vocabulary. Sometimes less is more.

This is the reason why Biggie's vocals have a timeless appeal. His rhymes are not dependent on any style or flow. A lotta joints he's done never sound dated. Because he never wrote shit down, his rhymes have a spontaneity that made for a great vocal performance.

Intense rhymes on songs like Somebody Got To Die required tracks that could create a *mood*. This is where Puff, the Hitmen and our engineers come in.

Go to your playlist and cue up *Who Shot Ya*. Focus on the music. (I know it's hard 'cause the rhymes are so good). David Porter's *I'm Afraid the Masquerade Is Over* sample anchors the track. Then there are the drums that keep things moving. Piano key accents intensify things. Puff's hype intro creates anticipation for Biggie's rhymes the same way Danny Ray warmed the crowd up for James Brown. He jumps in at the precise moment and uses an old Gamble and Huff trick---he hits you with the title first: *WHO SHOT YA!* As he goes into his rhyme, his vocals are doubled up, emphasizing certain lyrics whenever he is kicking something powerful. The music drops out for a second. It creates an aura of suspense---FUCKIN' WITH BIG/IT AINT SAFE!. In the background, Faith's moans weave in and out of the track giving it a morbid feel.

For five minutes and twenty seconds, the song plays out like a movie scene before climaxing into a bloody skit that visually revisits the entire theme of the song---a chilling instant replay doing double duty as a morbid crime scene

When people heard this, they went crazy. They just *knew* it was about Pac when in fact it was recorded way before all the drama. That says a lot about Biggie's talent as an emcee. You just can't pull an old joint outta the vault and drop it on the masses and hope it sticks. That's wishful thinking. Biggie painted vivid pictures and the producers and engineers provided the perfect canvas, producing a classic joint that still rocks. Think about it. *That record is almost twenty-five years old!*

Daddy's House was Biggie's kingdom. He held court with his homies there plus it was always food, liquor and women. One time a chick in a skimpy outfit was at the session. Biggie enters the booth to do his vocals. Next thing I know, she ends up in the booth with him. For a split second, Biggie is caught off guard. That was rare for him. He quickly regained his composure. *"What's up ma? Oh, it's like thaaaat?* Moans and groans erupted from a loudspeaker transforming the control room into one of Biggie's skits.

Big played hard but he worked even harder. The hits were piling up. In just three or four years he racked up a catalog of hot songs that surpassed the average rapper's career.

There was Mary's *Real Love* remix. The *Dolly Baby* joint with Super Cat then his first single *Party and Bullshit*. He had the streets locked with hardcore records like *Dreams, The What? Who Shot Ya* and *Unbelievable*. Radio was banging *Big Poppa, Juicy* and *One More Chance*. His verse on Craig Mack's *Flava In Ya Ear* was fire. Big was also part owner of Undeas Records. His label hit a home run straight out the gate. Junior Mafia's debut album went gold on strength of platinum and gold singles *Get Money* and *Player's Anthem*. He masterminded Lil Kim's Junior Mafia spinoff album *Hard Core* which quickly went gold. It would hit platinum in only eight months. Producers usually stuck a rapper in the middle of an R&B song, Big batted leadoff on Total's *Can't You See* and made that joint hot, giving them a gold single. Big could just be on the hook and still make it hot. He did records with Michael Jackson *and* Jay-Z. His *Ready to Die* album was double platinum. Now he was working on songs for his upcoming album *and* Puff's solo album. He had accomplished so much for a cat who was just 23 years old.

The world was Big's oyster. He lived big. He spent big. He was moving fast. Maybe too fast. He had gotten into a few legal scrapes. What finally slowed him down was an accident on the New Jersey Turnpike. Big never drove so his people always took him around. While his man Lil Cease was driving, he lost control of the car in the pouring rain. Cease lost most of his front teeth and Big broke his leg. As he rested up, producers were making their mark with their version of the Bad Boy flavor. Puff's master strategy ensured Bad Boy stayed ahead of the curve even though we had our critics.

As Big was putting in work and going through his issues, Pac was a raging timebomb. After he got shot, he went to prison on a rape charge. Having exhausted all his resources, he was in a tight spot. Suge Knight bailed him out and he aligned himself with Death Row Records. His fury was without boundaries or restrictions. He was calling out rappers like Nas and Mobb Deep. Bad Boy always remained in the crossfire. Just like Big, Pac was prolific too. He was dropping bombs all over the place. In two and half years he recorded *three* albums He followed up *Me Against The World* with *All Eyes On Me,* a double album that featured everything from huge radio records to battle rhymes targeting New York's hottest rappers. *Makavelli* was around the corner. The fans were loving him.

With Suge and the Death Row crew backing him up, Pac was making heated statements in the press who ate the whole thing up. He was on the warpath. Every party, event and award show turned into a potential warzone. Traveling back and forth between LA and New York on business was risky. Bodyguards were an absolutely a must.

Where I'm From: Growing Up Hip Hop

Looking back at that time between 1995 and 1996, it was a blur. I wonder how everybody got so much work done during that crazy time. When Tupac was killed in Vegas, hip hop stood still for a minute. Then it turned into a cauldron of drama. It turned the heat up even more.

Traveling became more dangerous. It was not just crazy in New York or in LA, it was just as wild in other places too. A month after Tupac's death, Miami was hosting the annual How Can I Be Down? music conference. If you were in the business, it was the place to be. Not for me. My friends Fritz and Gary pressured me to go. *"Ron, you don't wanna miss this, you need to be there."* I finally broke down and booked a ticket. Diddy had rented a mansion to do a photo shoot for his upcoming album. He was rolling out his campaign strategy to take over radio. Snippets of new Bad Boy songs were being played everywhere.

There were parties all over South Beach. Uncle Luke from 2 Live Crew had a set we could not miss. When we pulled up, the joint was at full capacity and people were still bum rushing the spot. Amongst the hectic crowd I spotted Wolf standing by the door. He was Puff's man from back in the day. He had a reputation for being heavy in the streets. He was holding Puff down. When he saw me, he pushed mad people to the side and pulled me in the club along with him.

Where I'm From: Growing Up Hip Hop

When I got inside it was like a music video come to life. Mad strippers were on stage. Cash was raining from the sky like manna from heaven. Everyone was having a wonderful time. Things got tense when Wu Tang's Ol' Dirty Bastard got on stage. He bobbed and weaved through the crowd in a drunken haze. Queens rapper Akinyele was in the spot. When Dirty bumped into Ak onstage, he was unapologetic. *"Fuck Akineleye!* As they pushed and shoved each other gunshots went off draining the club in an instant. We ran for the exit. *What the hell am I doing here?*

The next night was more chill. The next day, a young lady caught my eye in a club. I asked her to dance. Her name was Shay. She was from Brooklyn. As we got to know each other, I found out that Moms was her junior high school teacher back in the day. I learned that our birthdays were four days apart.

I thought it would be perfect for us to celebrate once we got back to New York. Shay and I hit it off and we hung out a few more times. Shay was a lot of fun. We became inseparable. Soon we were best friends. I brought her to parties, and sometimes she would sit in on recording studio sessions. Soon the trek from Mount Vernon to Brooklyn became a bit much, so eventually I moved into Shay's brownstone. Derickson always used to tell me to never be afraid to walk up and talk to a woman. I guess he was right!

Where I'm From: Growing Up Hip Hop

Track Twenty-Two
<u>Scrambling</u>

I wasn't in the studio when Big recorded his soon to be classic vocals for *Hypnotize*, but when I finally heard his voice booming through the control room, I melted. I thought to myself, *he did it again.* I didn't know it at the time but Big sat down the entire time he did the session.

When I saw him later, he was in a wheelchair and his people had to help him get around. Soon he moved to crutches and then finally a cane. He took his condition in stride. He even made a rhyme about it: *I used to be strong as ripple, B/till Lil' Cease crippled me.* After three months of being laid up in the hospital and another six in physical therapy, Big was back. Puff's prophecy was coming true. All those tracks we recorded in Trinidad were being shaped into actual songs. There was enough for a double album. Deric came up with the great idea to create a skit using *Ready to Die's* songs to kick off the new album. The energy was high.

The playa hating did not end with Tupac's tragic death. Bad Boy was still taking shots. Big was being counted out, but he was not going down though without a fight. You could hear it in his rhymes. *"I'm flamin' gats/aimin' at/the maniacs/who put/my name in raps."* Puff had laid low, taking the high row throughout all the beefs. Now he was spitting venom on joints like *Long Kiss Goodnight* and *My Downfall*, as Big's high-octane hype man.

I recorded my three best tracks on a Maxell cassette tape and scheduled a listening session with Diddy in the midi room. He listened to about three seconds of each track and passed on all of them. *"I need something else, playboy."* Puff had a picky ear, but I was growing tired of him passing on my tracks

By the time I left LA and came back to New York, I had come into my own as a producer. My production style was dramatic and inspired by the film scores from the 1970s like *Enter the Dragon* and *The French Connection*. These films had thrilling fight and car chase scenes set to music that was dark and intense.

Other producers were just focused on making hot beats. I was out to create *action-packed* movie soundtracks and film scores. That's the word Deric used when he was making fun of me for the way I created my beats. Puffy didn't like my sound at all. It made it harder for me to place tracks on the Bad Boy artists.

I realized after a while that if I needed to eat, I would have to change my sound to fit the vibe Puff was looking for. I started paying attention to what was winning and what I thought he would gravitate to. In the end, Puff still passed on my tracks and I ended up building a library of beats. I had so many I could call the DAT tape "Rejected by Bad Boy."

Puff had a vision for Mase's music, and it wasn't the "Murder Mase" hardcore style he was originally known for. My track *Wanna Hurt Mase* was the first song we recorded for his *Harlem World* album. He loved it. Puff hated the lyrical content and buried the record at the end of the album while frontloading *Harlem World* with more radio-friendly music.

I started going to other Bad Boy artists. I had nothing to lose. Black Rob and Mase were the newest acts on the roster but they hadn't recorded anything, so I started slipping them tracks. One of them contained a David Bowie sample of *Let's Dance*. When Mase heard it, his eyes lit up. *"I gotta have this."* We scheduled a session and after he laid down his verses, Biggie heard the beat and volunteered to do the chorus. He flipped the hook from a Lisa Stansfield record. Deric pulled me aside. He wasn't keen on giving Mase the track. I objected. *"Yo, I'm giving this track to Mase, yo. A nigga gotta eat. It's not like I'm getting any work right now. I'm going to let them record my shit, who knows what will come out of it. They're loving my tracks, so I'll let them record them."*

Puff walked in the studio and listened to the completed track. You could see the wheels turning in his head. He re-recorded Mase's original verses and kept Big on the hook. As I left the studio that night,

Where I'm From: Growing Up Hip Hop

Big's baritone followed me out the door all the way down 44th Street *"Been around the world and ayaiyaiay/we been playa hatin...."*

March rolled around and Bad Boy was ramping up for *Life After Death*'s release. *Hypnotize* was picking up steam. It was all over the radio. Of course, Puff had already thought of a master plan to put nothing but platinum in Bad Boy's hand. *Hypnotize* wasn't going to be a single release. He wanted to build up demand for the album.

First week-sales would be huge. The video for the record was crazy. Puff upped the ante, pushing conventional music video concepts over a cliff. He and Big were down in Florida, clad in silk Versace print shirts on a speedboat drinking champagne. The joint explodes into helicopter and car chases. Puff drives a Bentley Azure backwards for blocks while Big is kicking rhymes, calm cool and collected. Big plays up his injury to comic effect, hobbling towards the car trying to get away from assassins. As Puff jumps out of the moving car, Big drives the car backwards from the passenger seat with one hand on the steering wheel while his cane is on the gas.

That video would become a game changer. It would set the tone for future videos to come. Big came up with a dope hook that put the record over the top. When Pam flipped the chorus from *La Di-Da-Di*, it transformed my track into instant ear candy.

I was having a great year. Tracey Lee's *The Theme* was killing it everywhere. TV. Daytime radio. Hip hop mix shows. The backstory behind the record is crazy. Everyone involved with the record went to Howard University.

Back in '95, Tracey passed me his demo. I gave it to Carl from Shai who eventually signed him. He ended up sitting on Tracey for a year and nothing was happening for him.

In addition to working on music, Tracey was studying to be a lawyer. He found a loophole to get out of the contract. I hooked him up with Deric who put him down with Bystorm Entertainment run by Howard alum Mark Pitts. He signed Tracey to a production deal with Deric, pulling me in to produce three records for Tracey's debut album.

I remember being glued to the TV in between sessions checking for breaking news on the Tupac shooting in Vegas. Deric provided a skeleton of ideas kicking things off. I took it from there. I tightened up Malcolm McLaren's *World Famous* and Pieces of A Dream's *Mt. Airy Groove*. I took my time. I wanted to get it right. I was driving Deric crazy. He could not understand why it was taking me so long to finish the track.

Deric nearly pulled all the hairs out of his head. *"Ron, come on man! You killin' me right now"*. Two hours later, it was the same thing *"Yo my nigga, what are you doing? Come on dog, you taking too long."* I blocked D out. I had to make sure it was right because my name was going to be on this record.

In the end, it was all good. It took a few years, but Tracey finally had his moment. He booked passage on the Howard hip hop underground railroad. The record was a success. He made it to the Promised Land.

I made another dope record for Tracey called *Big Will*. I wanted to use Minnie Riperton's *Completeness* but couldn't clear the sample, so I played it over. Mark Pitts got Charisse Rose from the R&B duo Changing Faces to come in and duplicate Minnie's haunting whistle register and soprano vocal. Instead of a usual freestyle, Tracey kicked an ill storyline joint that was fire.

Meanwhile at Bad Boy, things were changing for me. Puff was finally on my side. *"Yo! that's it, we got it...we got it, I'm loving you right now!"* I was finally making headway with Puff, thanks to a remix.

I got a call from Bad Boy's project coordinator, Latrice Shaw. Her job was linking producers with outside projects. She had an opportunity for me. *"Ron, I got a call from Rick Brown at Elektra. Puffy's contracted to do a remix for MC Lyte's Cold Rock A Party but you can take a shot at it."* I picked up a copy of Lyte's acapella vocals from Latrice and headed home to work and called Deric. As soon as I finished, I shot back to the city and headed for Rick's office in the Atlantic Records building near Rockefeller Center.

Rockefeller Center.

Where I'm From: Growing Up Hip Hop

I was mad excited. I was sure we were good for the placement. Rick listened to the remix and shook his head. *"Ron, I like it but that's not what we are looking for."* I walked out of his office disappointed. I was not getting work at Bad Boy and now this! Then it hit me. *Puffy wouldn't listen to my tracks because I wasn't making them in the midi room.* I was dejected. I headed home but decided to stop by Daddy's House instead. When I got there, MC Lyte and a some industry heavy hitters are talking to Puff. I recognized Merlin Bobb, Atlantic's head of A&R and Drew Dixon, who I knew from Def Jam. Puffy was trying to explain how he was going to pull off Lyte's remix after taking an advance payment from Elektra.

I saw an opening. *"Yo, I see that you are working on the remix, I got something for you that I think you will like."* Puff gave me an urgent look and pulled me into the midi room. I handed him the DAT tape of the remix that I worked on. He was ecstatic. *"Do you have the floppy disks with you?"* I told them they were at home. He put his hand on my shoulder. *"Playboy, from now on you need to be prepared. Go home and get the disk, we are recording the vocals tonight!"*

I jumped in my Accord and jetted back to Mount Vernon. My adrenaline was racing. I got a project, lost a project and got it back all in a single day. I was doing a joint for MC Lyte! Mount Vernon was thirty minutes from the city. I made it in twenty-five. I grabbed the disk and rushed back down Henry Hudson Parkway back to Daddy's House.

Two weeks later the remix was on BET. I had two hot joints pumping on the radio. It was a perfect setup for *Hypnotize*! Things were looking up. I ran into Rick at a party a few weeks later. He told me I almost didn't make the cut on the remix credits, but he caught the error and added my name. From that point on, I stayed on Bad Boy to make sure everything was tight.

Where I'm From: Growing Up Hip Hop

MC Lyte and Amen-Ra

MC Lyte, Amen-Ra and DJ K Rock

Where I'm From: Growing Up Hip Hop

Tracy Lee reciting rhymes while working on the "Many Faces" album

Where I'm From: Growing Up Hip Hop

Track Twenty-Three
<u>Life After Death</u>

"Hey Ron! is it true that Biggie is dead?" An early morning phone call pulled me from a deep sleep. I felt like someone doused me with ice water. *"Turn on the radio! It's on Mr. Magic right now!"* I turned to WBLS, Magic's voice was low and somber. *"It's official. The Notorious B.I.G has passed away. I repeat, the Notorious B.I.G has passed away."* Big was in Cali promoting *Life After Death*. He also performed at a tape-delayed broadcast of the Soul Train Awards. He also won Best Rap Video for *Hypnotize*.

Instead of leaving for a scheduled flight to London the next day, Big attended an industry afterparty that weekend. The place was crazy packed to capacity and the police shut it down early. As Big and his crew were leaving, a car pulled up next to his truck and sprayed it with bullets. Big was pronounced dead nearly an hour later. It was a tragedy. I replayed the details in my mind. I just couldn't believe it. Pac had died the same way just six months ago. My last memory of Big was watching him sit on a stool in the Neve Room singing the chorus to one of my tracks.

Where I'm From: Growing Up Hip Hop

Big and Pac's stories will be linked forever. Their lives and careers were locked in a passionate dance radiating the heat of intense drama. Supportive onlookers cheered them on. Haters and critics dismissed them with a screw faced sneer. Their legacy is a Greek tragedy cloaked in poison's fatal irony. Two young brothers born a year apart with aspirations to rap. Success would come early for them both. Before long, their friendship turned to rivalry as their careers intersected, overlapping each other at dizzying speeds that even the most skilled driver would struggle to manipulate.

People pointed to Big and Pac's death as examples of what was wrong with hip hop. Violence has always lurked in the shadows of the music business. Peel back the pristine layers of R&B, rock, jazz and pop and you will find it.

I'll let you in on a secret. There was no blueprint for this rap shit. We were young cats trying to find a way to channel our creative expressions into a career.

There were no veteran industry mentors to guide us. They were too busy either going for self or looking down their nose at the next generation nipping at their heels. We were never provided with instructions on how to handle career false starts and disappointments or how to avoid bad deals and contracts. No one was there to counsel us on how youthful pride and bravado could erode into reckless arrogance.

Where I'm From: Growing Up Hip Hop

The grind was serious. There was no time to sit back and enjoy success, it was all about trying to *maintain* it. There were exceptions but for the most part, we had to learn this game on our own. We made up the rules as we went along and learned from our mistakes, often in the public eye.

People took the loss of Big hard. They loved his fly talk and "ashy-to-classy" narratives that spoke of his desire to secure his family. He was respected because he took Brooklyn along for the ride.

Big was the fly cat in the jewels but underneath it all, he was hip hop's everyman. His size fourteen Timberlands kicked in the systemic door of poor self-image that held us captive for years. Three decades after James Brown's *I'm Black and I'm Proud*, Big issued an official pardon that freed us all: *"Heartthrob never/fat, black, ugly as ever/however, I stay Coogi down to the socks/rings and watch/filled with rocks"*

Bad Boy was in full force at Big's funeral and wake. Streets were blocked off as celebrities and New York came to say their final goodbyes. At the service Faith serenaded Big, wailing away with such passion it gave me chills. It took me back to the Trinidad days when Faith was pregnant. I remember walking her from the beach back to the car when she was nauseous. Their relationship was tumultuous, but she held her head like the classy lady she was. Biggie looked grand in his casket. He was dressed in a fly suit just like the Detroit players he rapped about.

Where I'm From: Growing Up Hip Hop

It was a very sad moment and critical time for Bad Boy. Our label cornerstone was gone forever. After two days or so, it was back to life. Back to reality. Puffy didn't skip a beat and was ready to move forward. His first single *Can't Nobody Hold Me Down* was all over radio. He got together with Nashiem, and Carlos to make a hot track. They sampled *The Message* and beefed it up with heavy basslines and drums. They flipped the hook from *Break My Stride*, an eighties pop song.

The joint sold like crazy. It nearly went triple platinum. It was the first Bad Boy joint that introduced the world to Mase. Of course. there was an elaborate video to go with the song. It really played up Puff and Mase's onscreen chemistry.

After tossing a few names around for his album, Puff settled on *No Way Out*. It set the mood we were in to keep things rolling after Big's death. A few ideas were scrapped as we searched for the right tribute song for Big. They tried on a few things for size. Stevie created a track built around *I Miss You*, a classic Philly Soul record with a soulful Teddy Pendergrass that sounded like a vocal teardrop. Faith sang the hook. Because the song was too slow, Puff and Stevie used *Every Step You Take (I'll Be Watching You)* by The Police. Puff was locked and loaded, ready launch his assault on radio.

By the time we got to work, *Hypnotize* had been out for a few weeks. It was scheduled to be a promo-only release to push the album but after Big passed, Bad Boy released it as single.

Hypnotize's climb was patched into my direct line. My phone was starting to ring once it got out that I produced the record. I received a call from MBK, a small production company looking for producers. They had a young female singer signed to the company but didn't know what to do with her.

The singer was looking to incorporate hip hop style production in her music. After she had heard *Hypnotize*, she wanted to meet me. She and her boyfriend showed up at my doorstep ready to work. I dug through my crate of records and found a nice Isaac Hayes break that I thought would be cool for her to sing to. As I was working on the beat, she played around on my keyboard. The beat was cool, but I felt something was missing. If I could recreate the live string arrangements, then I could take this track over the top.

I reached out to MBK to put me in touch with Isaac, who was doing radio for Kiss FM at the time. I figured if I was going to do the project, it made sense to collaborate with the originator.

A few days later we were sitting in a conference room at Sony Records with Isaac. His focus is on the singer during the entire meeting and I'm invisible to him. It's clear he only wants to work with her. He's not looking for a package deal.

For the next hour, I picked Isaac's brain and asked him about string arrangements. Nothing panned out for me. The singer and her partner retreated underground. They emerged a few years later with a massive album and a huge single that blew her career up. Every time I heard it on the radio, I felt privileged to have had a front seat and witness the gifted brilliance that was Alicia Keys.

Where I'm From: Growing Up Hip Hop

Where I'm From: Growing Up Hip Hop

The drums from Hypnotize stored on this floppy disk

The magic DAT

Where I'm From: Growing Up Hip Hop

Track Twenty-Four
<u>The Magic DAT</u>

I am sitting in a small office in Midtown plotting my exit strategy. I look across a table at my attorneys Reginald Ossè and Ed Woods. I am glad I have them on my team. When I signed my contract a year ago, I went outside the network and got with Reggie and Ed. Deric and I were their first clients. We launched our careers together.

These brothers aren't your average legal team. Ossè is from Brooklyn, the son of a Haitian immigrant striver who made it her goal to expose him to a bigger world. He navigated the rugged terrain of polarizing neighborhoods when he was bused out to a school in Ridgewood, Queens. He was a creative type like me but ended up at Georgetown studying law. After a stint at Def Jam, Ossè set up shop with Ed.

Ed was from Farmer's Boulevard in Queens. He honed his sharp legal mind navigating hectic situations while working at his father's cab stand. I never had to worry about any conflict of interest with Ossè and Woods. They weren't about playing both sides, trying to juggle Bad Boy's best interests and mine. They also weren't part of the web of thirsty service providers standing in line, ready to be of service as soon as the ink from my contract was dry. I had heard about this game many times.

Between the labels, lawyers, accountants, the car leasing agents, realtors and business managers, it was like my great-aunt's Harlem all over again. Advance money and royalty check percentages sent their kids to college. It happened to countless rappers, singers and producers entering a complex world more ruthless than the streets they left behind.

Ossè and Woods weren't ambulance chasers following the money. They were the real deal. Together, we were Brooklyn and Queens guys who were young and hungry. Brothers from other mothers. Distant relatives all cut from hip hop's umbilical cord. Ossè sees the stress on my face as I let loose. *"Things ain't going right for me man. I'm ready to leave. I ain't getting no real work here. I have a hot single on the radio, I think I can ride this wave and do my own thing now."*

I had signed a five-year deal with Bad Boy. I had a one-year option to renew if I earned seventy-five thousand dollars. The second year doubled that amount. The longer I stayed, there was potential that the money would get bigger. I had a loophole that would allow me to break my contract early. So far, I had only made about ten thousand, which meant that I could leave anytime. Ossè suggested that I set up a courtesy meeting with Puff and inform him of my intent to leave.

It was hard trying to nail Puffy down. He was never at the record company. He hated sitting behind a desk. He left the day to day stuff for guys like Kirk Burrowes to handle. Kirk was a day-one Bad Boy member from back in the days when Puff ran the label from out of his house in Scarsdale.

The best place to find him was at Daddy's House. It was his second home. Puff was a master multi-tasker. He would always have more than one thing going on. I would usually wait around a bit and come back later. This time I stayed put. If it meant hanging around for hours until the sun came up, that was what I was prepared to do.

I found my opening the next day during a session for *I'll Be Missing You*. We headed for the Neve Room. I looked him in the eye and went in. *"Puff man, I've been here a whole year and haven't gotten any songs placed with you yet. I feel like I'm just as good as any producer that you have signed to Bad Boy."*

Puffy stopped me mid-sentence. *"Hold up, hold up. I've been checking you out for a minute, and I know you got that heat. I wanna change things for you. I'm gonna make you rich. Let's start fresh. I want you to go home and put all your hottest beats on DAT tape, and I am going to change your life."* I looked into his eyes. He looked sincere. Up until this time, I worked from home, building up my music stash. I played my position as a Hitman. I helped in the studio and submitted hot tracks. I busted my ass, but the coach was not putting me in the game. I was tired of being the twelfth man on the roster. It was time to come off the bench or move on.

I decided to take a chance and take Puff's word. I went home and put all the hottest tracks I had worked on for the past year onto DAT tape and handed it in the next day. From that point on, things changed. *"Yo Ron, track this one here, I want this one too. This one would be hot for Faith. Yo, I need that other joint for my album."* I couldn't believe it! My songs were getting placed with all the Bad Boy artists. There were moments where I would walk into Daddy's House and all my tracks were being played in every room. Engineers were hard at work. Artists and songwriters were doing their thing to my music. It was all because of my *digital audio tape.*

What was so important about this magic DAT? When Puffy told me to go home and put all my best work on that DAT and give it to him, it transformed my life *and* the label. It contained all the songs he had passed on and quite a few others that I was reluctant to play him. One day after I gave Puff the DAT, it seemed like hit records fell from the sky, left and right. The DAT doubled as a way for Puff to showcase hot music to potential clients and as a quick solution for my occasional producer's block. If I couldn't come up with anything, I would pull tracks from the DAT. Puffy would tell me not to touch it unless he knew about it. He would play it for the Bad Boy artists and outside talent looking for hit containing our signature sound.

We had heavy hitters like Brian McKnight, LL Cool J, Boyz II Men and others lined up but sometimes it got crazy. When Jive Records cut Deric and I a nice hefty check without hearing any tracks, my back was against the wall, so I went back to the DAT and pulled a track from it.

When R&B group Imajin dropped their first single it was all on New York radio, I got a call from Puffy. I met him at his office afterwards. He wasn't happy about me going against his wishes. I told him I wouldn't do it again, not knowing that one final trip to the well would give me a record that would solidify my status as a producer.

Where I'm From: Growing Up Hip Hop

Reggie Osse (Combat Jack) Amen-Ra and Ed Woods of Osse & Woods, Esq.

Where I'm From: Growing Up Hip Hop

Amen-Ra and Puff Daddy

Carlos Broady, Amen-Ra, Puff Daddy, J-Dub and Stevie J

Where I'm From: Growing Up Hip Hop

Inside Daddy's House midi room

Where I'm From: Growing Up Hip Hop

Yogi, Stevie J and Mike Patterson

Jay Dub and Puff Daddy

Where I'm From: Growing Up Hip Hop

D-Dot, Puffy and Younglord

Carlos Broady, Nashiem and Amen-Ra

Notorious B.I.G. and Hassan (Sonny) Pore

Where I'm From: Growing Up Hip Hop

Where I'm From: Growing Up Hip Hop

Where I'm From: Growing Up Hip Hop

Billboard HOT 100 SINGLES
MAY 17, 1997

THIS WEEK	LAST WEEK	2 WKS AGO	WKS ON CHART	TITLE — PRODUCER (SONGWRITER)	PEAK POSITION	ARTIST — LABEL & NUMBER/PROMOTION LABEL
				★★★ No. 1 ★★★		
1	1	1	4	HYPNOTIZE — D.ATKINS,S.JORDAN,J.OLIVIER,C.WALLACE,S.JONES,R.BRISTOL,R.LAWRENCE,F.BARRETT,A.JOHNSON,J.NEW,K.NITTY,A.LYLES,C.BROWN) 3 weeks at No. 1	1	◆ THE NOTORIOUS B.I.G. (C) (D) (T) (X) BAD BOY 79092/ARISTA
2	6	16	8	MMMBOP — THE DUST BROTHERS (I.HANSON,T.HANSON,Z.HANSON)	2	◆ HANSON (C) (D) MERCURY 574261
3	7	7	12	RETURN OF THE MACK — M.MORRISON,P.CHILL (M.MORRISON,P.CHILL)	3	◆ MARK MORRISON (C) (D) (T) (X) ATLANTIC 84868
4	2	3	25	YOU WERE MEANT FOR ME ● — B.KEITH,P.COLLINS (JEWEL,S.POLTZ)	2	◆ JEWEL (C) (D) ATLANTIC 87021
5	5	4	10	FOR YOU I WILL (FROM "SPACE JAM") ● — D.FOSTER (D.WARREN)	4	◆ MONICA (C) (D) ROWDY/WARNER SUNSET 87003/ATLANTIC
6	4	5	12	I WANT YOU ● — C.FISHER (D.HAYES,D.JONES)	4	◆ SAVAGE GARDEN (C) (D) (T) (X) COLUMBIA 78503
7	3	2	17	CAN'T NOBODY HOLD ME DOWN ▲ — SEAN "PUFFY" COMBS,C.THOMPSON (S.COMBS,M.BETHA,S.JORDAN,M.OLIVER,J.BARNES,M.C.ROGERS,W.PRESTON,N.WHITFIELD,S.ROBINSON)	1	◆ PUFF DADDY (FEATURING MASE) (C) (D) (T) (X) BAD BOY 79083/ARISTA
8	8	9	8	WHERE HAVE ALL THE COWBOYS GONE? ● — P.COLE,P.COLE	8	◆ PAULA COLE (C) (D) (T) (V) (X) IMAGO 17327/WARNER BROS.
9	9	8	8	HARD TO SAY I'M SORRY ● — BABYFACE,P.FOSTER (P.CETERA,D.FOSTER)	8	◆ AZ YET FEATURING PETER CETERA (C) (D) (T) (V) (X) LAFACE 24723/ARISTA
10	12	15	10	I BELONG TO YOU (EVERY TIME I SEE YOUR FACE) ● — G.BAILLERGEAU,V.MERRITT (R.IRVING,V.MERRITT,G.BAILLERGEAU)	10	◆ ROME (C) (D) (V) RCA 64759

THIS WEEK	LAST WEEK	2 WKS AGO	WKS ON CHART	TITLE — PRODUCER (SONGWRITER)	PEAK POSITION	ARTIST — LABEL & NUMBER/PROMOTION LABEL
49	46	38	20	LET IT GO (FROM "SET IT OFF") — K.CROUCH (K.CROUCH,G.MCKINNEY,R.PENNON)	25	◆ RAY J (C) (D) (M) (T) (X) EASTWEST 64206/EEG
50	53	68	3	UNTIL I FIND YOU AGAIN — R.MARX (R.MARX)	50	◆ RICHARD MARX (C) (D) (V) CAPITOL 58633
51	49	44	15	GANGSTAS MAKE THE WORLD GO ROUND — ICE CUBE (ICE CUBE,MACK 10,W.C.,C.SAMSON,T.BELL,L.CREED)	40	◆ WESTSIDE CONNECTION (C) (D) (T) LENCH MOB 53264/PRIORITY
52	57	67	6	COME ON — D.ALLAMBY (B.LAWRENCE,D.ALLAMBY)	52	◆ BILLY LAWRENCE FEATURING MC LYTE (C) (D) (M) (T) (X) EASTWEST 64239/EEG
53	51	53	3	IF TOMORROW NEVER COMES — P.PETTIS,H.LEE (K.BLAZY,G.BROOKS)	51	◆ JOOSE (C) (D) (X) FLAVOR UNIT/EASTWEST 64199/EEG
54	83	—	2	ESPN PRESENTS THE JOCK JAM — P.EDMONDS,R.CASTOLDI (VARIOUS)	54	VARIOUS ARTISTS (C) (D) TOMMY BOY 7780
55	54	46	9	GHETTO LOVE ● — J.DUPRI (DA BRAT,J.DUPRI,R.PARKER,A.GOLDBERG,B.GORDY,A.MIZELL,F.PERREN,D.RICHARDS,T.RANDAZZO,B.WEINSTEIN,L.STALLMAN)	16	◆ DA BRAT FEATURING T-BOZ (C) (D) (T) (V) (X) SO SO DEF 78527/COLUMBIA
56	58	58	5	CALL ME — DRE,YELLA (ANDRE YOUNG,A.MCDONALD,A.LYLES)	56	◆ LE CLICK (C) (D) (T) (X) LOGIC 45779/MCA
57	55	51	11	HEAD OVER HEELS — ALLURE,P.POKE & TONE (M.COREY,N.JONES,B.BARNES,J.C.OLIVER,M.WILLIAMS,J.ROLTE)	35	◆ ALLURE FEATURING NAS (C) (D) (T) TRACK MASTERS 78522/CRAVE
58	52	52	6	JAZZY BELLE ● — ORGANIZED NOIZE (A.PATTON,A.BENJAMIN,A.PATTON)	52	◆ OUTKAST (C) (D) (T) (X) LAFACE 24213/ARISTA
59	66	87	3	ONE NIGHT AT A TIME — T.BROWN,E.STRAIT (E.LEE,E.HILL,R.BOWLES,E.COOK)	59	GEORGE STRAIT (C) (D) (V) MCA 55457

254

Track Twenty-Five
Flying High

Hypnotize was a monster hit. The record sold a million copies and reached the Billboard top spot. I had officially arrived, and it sent a message to the industry, putting them on notice---I was a force to be reckoned with and was here to stay. *I Love You Baby* and *Been Around the World*---songs that Puff originally had passed on that I placed with Mase and Black Rob ended up going on Puff's album. Evidently, Puff had a change of heart because once he heard them, he added himself to the tracks by re-recording their second verses. It all worked out well because the mixture of their vocal tones made the joints stand out.

From that moment, my life changed. There was a check on the table for every track Puff picked. Because I was so hot, he made sure my first and second contractual years were filled with advances so there would be no room to negotiate an exit plan out of the management contract in the middle of my hot streak. Within thirty days, I had a hundred thousand dollars in my bank account! I was rolling. It was the first time I had ever seen that kind of money in such a short period of time.

In one month, I made more than both of my parents' combined salary. I was only thirty-one years old. I knew that things could only get better from that point.

It was time to reward myself. I hooked up with my man Hassan who turned me on to a jeweler. I bought a nice blue face Rolex with a bezel covered in diamonds.

I was ready to get rid of my Accord. I only had it for a year, but what the hell? I was visiting Moms in Queens and stopped by Silver Star Motors on Northern Boulevard. I had my eye on a Mercedes Benz S500. It was a top of the line model. As I checked the car out, no one would come and talk to me. When I found a salesman, he gave me the cold shoulder. *"Do you know how much this car costs? Don't waste my time."* When I walked into a BMW dealer in Manhattan, I was escorted straight to the showroom. I walked out with a black 740IL. The whip was fully loaded and was the first carl with a navigation system.

I had the jewels and the whip. Now it was time to upgrade my wardrobe. I copped fifteen pairs of Gucci shoes and sneakers of every kind. It felt good to finally get a taste of the good life. I spent most of my time with Shay and her daughter. Our bond was strengthening. We were becoming a family. Even though I was in Brooklyn now, I would still hit my brother off with a few hundred dollars for rent.

Where I'm From: Growing Up Hip Hop

A regular day for me would be hanging out with my buddies and going to industry parties to network and set up meetings. I kept my eyes on the prize though. I navigated the maze of traps set for industry cats with new money. I avoided guys like Bert Padell who were overrun with clients. I didn't want to mess with corporate firms charging steep prices that I had to make an appointment with to see them.

Slick Rick's DJ, Vance Wright turned me on to a cool accountant in the Scarsdale who taught me the ropes. Vance's family worked with Mr Romagnano for years. This worked in my favor. I was a premier client and they were always accessible to me. I stayed focused on making beats to keep the checks rolling in. I was making more on one song than most people made in a year.

People kept checking for my beats. My phone would not stop ringing. Records companies were lining up for my music. Bad Boys kept me abreast of the latest artists that wanted to work with me. Every time Puff selected a track from that DAT tape it was like pulling a rabbit out of a hat.

I reached back to one of my favorite songs, *Love's Holiday* by Change. I slowed down the pitch and Stevie added a bassline. It would end up on an R. Kelly album that sold seven million copies. I looped up James Brown's *Ants in My Pants (When I Need to Dance)*. I isolated the guitars and created a four-bar stutter intro to kick things off to capture the listener's ear. A keyboard riff gave the track a dramatic flair like the old Philly Soul and Isaac Hayes records. I put drums and a filtered bass underneath to make it bounce. Stevie's live bass tied things together. When singer Brian McKnight came calling, Puff gave him the track. It was Brian's first hit uptempo record. It ended up selling 600,000 copies.

Jive Records gave Deric and I a nice upfront advance to make a record for a Will Smith movie soundtrack. When Will moved over to a new label, the project went with him and the label reassigned it to other producers who flipped the Patrice Rushen's *Forget Me Nots* sample idea to create a similar type of track. They called it *Men in Black*. It sold over three million copies and was number one in fourteen countries. It helped push Will's album to ten million sold *and* he won a Grammy.

It was a perfect way to set off his solo career. It worked out for me too. I was able to keep the advance. It was the easiest thirty-five thousand I ever made.

I made a lot of hit records but my favorite track that I made around this time was one people may not be familiar with. It was a soundtrack type soulful track with hard drums and strings with rolling piano keys instead of the high energy radio records I was becoming known for. The track recreated the vibe of Gamble and Huff styled R&B songs like *Wake Up Everybody, Family Reunion* and *Be Thankful for What You Got*. I hired background singers to sing on the track to give the music a churchy feel. I tacked on rain sound effects to give the record a somber effect. Rappers Peter Gunz and Lord Tariq laced *My Time to Go* with powerful lyrics ripped from the pages of the book of their turbulent lives. The record came out great. We made a masterpiece.

As a Hitman team, we competed to see how many songs we could get placed on an album. *Now* it was about how many joints you could get on the radio. I was on a hot streak. I had mastered creating the right tracks for radio airplay, which translated into huge producer checks, publishing fees and royalties. While there was always enough work to go around, I usually got the call around this time. There was a little tension, but it was all love.

Old friends were starting to find me, and new friends were popping up. Cousins that I never knew I had found ways to get in contact with me. No matter who it was, it was the same old song. Everybody needed a loan. Every time I turned around; I was helping cats out of financial jams doing things like paying their bills. I paid rent too. It was all starting to add up. In the beginning, they might have had good intentions on paying me back but the more my name rang out and they *really* found out how well I was doing? *They didn't want to pay me back!* It left me with a bad taste in my mouth.

When I started turning down requests for money, some of my old crew got angry and did not speak to me for a while. I had to let them know it was not personal. It was not like I could keep a low profile. Before, I was just trying to stay afloat. Now, I was *soaring*. Bad Boy's music was everywhere.

When I was in my car, my songs were on the radio. If I was watching MTV or BET, our videos were in heavy rotation. I used to go to clubs just to hear how many of my joints were being played. I always left with a smile on my face. Even when it became a common thing, I never lost that feeling of satisfaction of having my music out in the forefront.

One of the things about being financially secure is that having money gives people time to focus on things they usually ignored when they were on the grind. Things like health and self-care. Because I was a vegetarian, I stayed on the slender side, so I was looking to tone up a bit. My man Flipper hooked me up with a great routine. He was a celebrity trainer who worked with industry guys like Puff and Chris Lighty. Flipper had me looking right. Things were coming together. My skin and body were on point. I had the Rolex. I had the gear and I had the whip. When I say I was shining yo, I was *shining*. It was just one more piece to the puzzle. I needed a house. I wanted a luxury home.

During a workout session, Flipper hooked me up with Chris who put me on to his realtor in West Orange. Nothing caught my eye at first, but when the realtor showed me a nice modern split-level that sat on a hill with a large front lawn, I knew it was for me. The house was airy with an open floor plan. Coming from my old home in

Queens, space was exactly what I wanted. Every room had a sunroof. The basement was spacious enough for me to build a large studio. After the papers were signed, Shay and I moved in. The neighborhood was nice.

It seemed like everyone from the music business lived in and around my neighborhood. Robert (Kool) Bell of Kool and the Gang lived a short drive away. Shay and I enjoyed spending time with Kool and his wife Sakinah. Hip Hop radio personality Ed Lover from Yo! MTV Raps lived nearby. He and Chris were next door neighbors. All the Fugees lived in Jersey too. Pras and Wyclef lived close. Lauryn and her producer Vada Nobles lived over in East Orange. So did James Mtume. Hip hop clothing designer Guy Wood lived across the street from me. Kay Gee from Naughty by Nature lived not too far. His son attended school with my step daughter Shayla. I would throw barbecues at the crib and invite them over. I would live in other places over the years, but I will never forget the fun times I had at my place at 15 McGuire Drive.

While I was settling into my suburban lifestyle in Jersey, Puff was taking the Hamptons by storm. He was already known for his lavish parties, but he took it up a notch when he bought a place in East Hampton and started throwing Fourth of July parties every year. Three or four years ago, guys like Russell and Andre would rent out a beach house together for the summer and throw huge parties. Puff took it to the next level.

Where I'm From: Growing Up Hip Hop

He laid down $2.5 million for a place on Hedges Banks Drive and *really* brought hip hop to the Hamptons. By now, he was the most popular cat in the music business. To get into a Puff party was like being invited to the White House. Everyone wanted to get in. He had a strict code in terms of what he wanted you to wear. If you did not comply, you might get turned away.

It was crazy to see people running around trying to get their outfit together for the event or begging security to be let in. *"Yo! Can you get me in?" "I'm sorry, ladies, you're not on the list."* Puff was like a pied piper. Everyone from industry people and fashion models to cats from the hood would be there. It was like Freaknik. We were there every year and always had a good time. There was food and music. Only a couple hundred people were invited. Some of the white folks in the neighborhood though didn't like it one bit. The Hamptons was considered exclusive. To see niggas walking around with Timbs and white tees driving around with loud music scared the shit out of them.

That summer, Deric and I were honored at a producers' luncheon hosted by the National Recording Academy Society. One of my musical heroes, James Mtume gave our introduction speech. It felt good to have Shay, her mom, Derickson and Moms there.

While Pops was proud of what I was doing, Moms was from the old school. She was about education and getting a good job. She really did not understand what I did to earn a living. She was happy for me though. Moms beamed with pride as industry people came up to me, congratulating me.

I turned away for a split-second and out of the corner of my eye, I saw Moms shaking. Her eyes did not look right. Body spasms caused her body to jerk back and forth. I called out to her, *"Mom…Mom… can you hear me? Are you alright?"* My heart sank as the paramedics took her away. She had a seizure. In a few years, she would have another one and then they would turn into mini strokes.

I wanted to end the year with a bang. I rented out the Cheetah Club and threw a party to celebrate my success. I invited all the A&R and record execs. It was a star-studded event. Everyone from the sports and entertainment world was there. Sylvia Rhone, Mike Tyson, Tyrese, Kedar Massenburg, Illyashah Shabazz and my labelmates Total. I was dressed to impress and ready to shine.

Usually, it was the record label that threw industry parties in support of their artists. The party cost a fortune, but I wanted to put the industry on notice that I was a force to be reckoned with in this game. The party was such a success that the local news channels came out to cover it. I don't smoke, but that was a night I definitely was on cloud nine.

I was still on a bit of a high the next day as I watched the news coverage of my party. I found out later that Puff had held a large press conference the same night as my party, promoting the launch of his brand-new restaurant. It was right across the street from Cheetah Club! When I saw Puff the next day, he didn't look happy. He had the same look on his face that he had when we first showed up at the studio after our rental car fiasco. It was like a scene out of the film Menace II Society. Puff was Bill Duke and I was Caine. Puff's icy glare said it all: *You know you done fucked up, right?* When he threw a Christmas party at Justin's for the Bad Boy staff two weeks later, he handed out expensive gifts to everybody. It was his way of expressing his appreciation for the year we had. Guess who was the only one left out? You guessed it right, *Me*. It was Puff's way of paying me back.

I'm not sure if Puff really felt like I was trying to compete with him that night. Maybe he thought that I had intentionally tried to take some of the attention away from his event. I didn't care. I wasn't going to let it get to me.

I had a great year and was anticipating many more in the future. I filed the situation away in my mind, reminding myself to continue to keep everything strictly business.

Amen-Ra and Mike Tyson

Amen-Ra and Tyrese Gibson

Amen-Ra and Ilyasah Shabazz (Malcolm X's daughter)

Merlin Bob, Amen-Ra and Sylvia Rhone

Amen-Ra and Total (Keisha and Kima)

Jeffrey Rolle, Amen-RA, Kelly Price and Ed Woods

Chilling with my brother Derrick (Lyburd) and his wife, Shinikwa

Amen-Ra and older brother Derickson

Where I'm From: Growing Up Hip Hop

Amen-Ra, Shayla and Shay

Amen-Ra

Where I'm From: Growing Up Hip Hop

At the A&R Producers Luncheon given by the Grammy Organization

NARAS Governor's Award

presented to
Ron Lawrence
New Horizons Award

For your outstanding
contributions to the
art of recording
June 23, 1998

A&R/PRODUCERS LUNCHEON

Deric Angelettie & Ron Lawrence

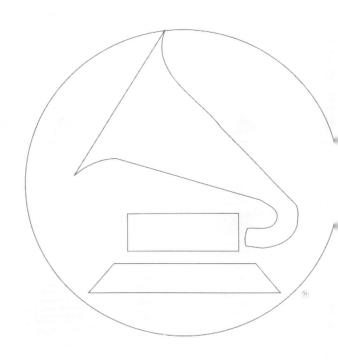

A&R/PRODUCERS LUNCHEON

*D*eric Angelettie and Ron Lawrence have burst upon the music scene with astounding success. The two have been charting since they attended Howard University and were known as The Mystery System and were producing records from their dorm room. The world of Hip Hop knows their earlier work as D.O.P. and Amen-Ra or, as they were collectively known, Two Kings in a Cipher (TKC).

In 1991, they released an album titled **From Pyramids to Projects** for Bahia/RCA Records. Two hits, **Movin' on Em** and **For the Brothers Who Ain't Here** jumped out from that CD. Their current success is no mystery, thanks to the flavorful jams they have produced for Puff Daddy, Boyz II Men, The Notorious B.I.G., MC Lyte and Brian McKnight, among others. Their chart-topping hits include Puff Daddy & Family's **All About Benjamins**, LL Cool J's **Phenomenon**, The Notorious B.I.G.'s **Hypnotize** and Brian McKnight's **You Should Be Mine**.

Angelettie and Lawrence are keeping up the pace with additional credits for JayZ, The Lox and LSG. And, they are scheduled to team up with stars such as Faith Evans, Jermaine Dupri and Jody Watley.

The team prides itself on its mutual honesty and for not stepping on each other's toes. Angelettie sees himself as street with Lawrence the technical person and music librarian. They want people to always know that this hit making duo can always produce a hot song. Angelettie and Lawrence believe that they are poised to take their work to another level. And, when this does happen, it certainly will be no mystery to their fans.

Where I'm From: Growing Up Hip Hop

Track Twenty-Six
<u>Money, Power & Respect</u>

One evening we were all gathered around the MPC-3000 drum machine inside the midi room at Daddy's House. We were suffering from producer's block. Whenever our creative juices ran dry, we kept people around who had kept a stash of records on deck. They helped spark ideas to keep our minds working. My Hurst homeboy Jay Garfield was hanging with us that night. He pulled out a copy of Dexter Wansel's *Time Is Slipping Away* album and handed it to Deric. I knew Dexter from my old Philly days. Back in Queens, DJs rocked his *Life on Mars* in the parks. I cued up *A New Beginning* and caught it on the snare.

Deric and I went back and forth all night, chopping up the sample until we got it tight. Early morning sapped our creative energy, leaving us with nothing but a naked chopped up sample with no drums, keyboards or anything added to it.

We didn't have an artist in mind when we created the track but whatever we created had to be attached to a recording budget of a

Bad Boy artist to justify use of studio time in Daddy's House midi room. Later, Deric took the track to the Lox. They liked it and Deric handled the recording of their vocals. A few weeks later I was lying in my bed and I received a phone call from Tony Maserati while he was mixing down the record. *"Ron, I'm having problems mixing the record because the track is too naked. Can you come down?"* When got to the studio I heard the song, I was impressed at how The Lox, Lil Kim and DMX all worked their magic on a track that was just a skeleton of a sample that D and I constructed.

I pulled out the cache of sounds that filled my floppy disks and got to work on the MPC-3000. Once the drums were laid down perfectly, I added the bass line from my Roland JV-1080 Module synthesizer. The track sounded good on the monster-sized stadium speakers in the SSL room during playback. I knew it was a hit. Puff walked in on the session and didn't respond in his normal way when I laced him. Instead he said, *"I'm not feeling the hook on that one."* It eventually grew on him. We called it *Money, Power and Respect*---it's from a famous line from the *Scarface* film.

Money, Power and Respect rocked the street, clubs and radio. My hot streak was intact but one of my next hits was a song that almost never happened.

Where I'm From: Growing Up Hip Hop

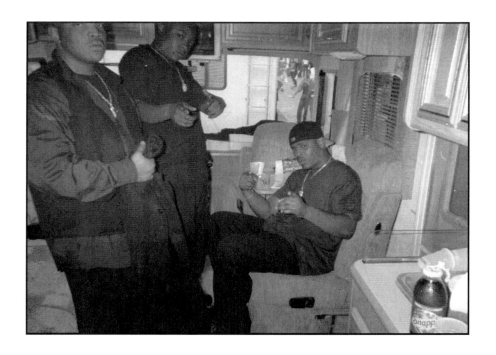

Where I'm From: Growing Up Hip Hop

Where I'm From: Growing Up Hip Hop

Track Twenty-Seven
<u>The Song That Almost Never Was</u>

One of my most memorable moments during that time was working on the LL Cool J *Phenomenon* album. During the week of Memorial Day, we booked studio time at the Hit Factory. Puff was in the middle of his weekly manicure when I showed up to the studio. Puff never missed his scheduled manicure, haircut or shape-up His barber Curtis was always ready with the clippers. He eventually built a salon in the lounge at Daddy's House. That joint even had a pool table in it.

Puff looked regal and majestic as his groomers hovered over him, tending to his needs. LL showed up with Violator manager Chris Lighty ready to work. Puff greeted LL but didn't move from his seat. *"What's up, playboy, almost done."*

LL didn't talk much but his body language spoke volumes. He paced around all hyper-like. He was kind of tight. The session was on his dime and the clock was ticking.

While Puff was finishing up, he asked me to play my tracks for LL and Chris. I pulled out my DAT tape and played him eleven tracks. LL was excited. He especially liked my track featuring a Creative

Source sample of *Who Is He (And What Is He to You)*. The track had a bouncy circular bass line that was dope. LL smiled and started rhyming to the beat.

"Do you have those recordings on disks?" Puff's voice filled the room. He was ready to work. I offered a weak "yes" and turned away. I wasn't sure I had it. I checked all my floppy disks and I couldn't believe it. The *one* song LL was tripping over, *I had decided to leave at home, today of all days.* Puff instructed me to record the beat onto 24 tracks. All the outboard equipment was laid out and the other equipment was ready to go. Back in those days recording equipment was rented by the hour and charged to an artist's budget. Time was money and a moment could not be wasted.

LL was amped and ready to work. *"How long will it take you to record the track?"* I tried to keep calm. *"Give me about an hour and thirty minutes."* I looked at my Rolex. My mind was racing. *It's after five now, how am I going to get the floppy disk in time?* At the time I was still in Mount Vernon--- forty minutes to an hour away in rush hour traffic.

As Puff, LL and Chris left to get something to eat, I took a deep breath and rested my head down against my MPC. I realized in order to complete this track I would have to recreate it immediately. I called around to various record stores to see who carried the Creative Source album the song was sampled from. I called everywhere. No one had it. I mentally braced myself to deliver the bad news to LL. I had dropped the ball and was in danger of making Puff, myself and the label look bad.

I decided to give it another shot. I called Tower Records in Greenwich Village downtown. They had the album on CD. I rushed out of the studio and flagged down a cab. We drove down Broadway through heavy traffic. I sat in the back gripping the seat, glaring at the gridlock ahead of me. I tried to mentally will them to pick up the pace and go faster. My heart was pounding.

By the time we got to Tower Records, an hour had passed. I rushed out of the cab and sprinted toward the revolving doors. I bought the CD and went outside to hail a cab. None would stop for me.

When a cab finally stopped, the driver passed me up to pick up a young white lady. I jumped in before she did. *"Take me to 57th Street."* The cab driver wouldn't move. He told me he was not going that way. *"I'm not getting out of this cab. You need to drive!"* We argued for five minutes until the driver finally gave in. As I headed back, I prepared myself for the backlash that I knew was sure to come.

As I walked into the studio, everyone got quiet. They all looked at me as I slowly walked in and sat down beside the MPC-300 drum machine. LL started screaming at the top of his lungs. *"YO DOG, WHAT ARE YOU DOING? YOU THINK THIS IS A JOKE? YOU WASTING MY STUDIO TIME AND NOT TAKING CARE OF*

BUSINESS?" OVER TWO HOURS HAVE GONE BY AND STILL AIN'T NOTHIN' DONE SINCE WE LEFT OUT OF HERE! WHAT THE HELL ARE YOU DOING?" LL was going in deep. *In too deep.*

This was a whole different cat from the humble dude Apollo, Hurby and I walked to the train station nearly fifteen years ago. I blocked out LL and went into a zone. I could see his mouth moving but I couldn't hear him.

Bruce Lee's words steered me through the turbulent waters of LL's bitter wrath. *A quick temper will make a fool of you soon enough. Mistakes are always forgivable, if one has the courage to admit them."* I removed my ego from the situation like a boulder blocking my path. I told myself, *L's not trying to play me. He's just passionate about his craft.*

I kept my cool and explained what happened. Puffy was cool with the situation as well. He always said to me that he did not care how things got done, if you can make it happen. LL was not as gracious. *"I don't care what you do, you bring a turntable, helicopter or an umbrella. Make sure things get done on time!"*

Later, Chris told me LL could be very temperamental. He assured me that he would be okay throughout the rest of the studio session. Later, Russell Simmons stopped through to pay a visit. I had never gotten a chance to meet him and we had a long conversation.

He gave me props and told me how much he had appreciated my contribution to LL's album.

I started to feel more at ease and went into work mode. Things ended up working out better by rebuilding the track. It sounded better than the original. After I recreated it, the engineer and I recorded the track. LL began writing his lyrics and recited them back to me as he sat on the couch.

Our earlier tension faded, and we swapped music stories. LL told me that he made the beats for *Big Ole Butt* and the original album version of *Jinglin' Baby*. I was amazed at how guys like LL and Rakim were great at making beats, but their skills were overshadowed by their prowess on the mike.

When we listened to the song during playback, we knew we had an instant hit. *Phenomenon* pushed the album to gold sales in only a month after its release. Two months later the album was platinum. In his book *I Make My Own Rules*, he talked about naming the album *Smithsonian*. The album ended up being called *Phenomenon*. I was proud to have had the opportunity to work with the GOAT. After the close call I had, I felt vindicated when the record was a success.

Where I'm From: Growing Up Hip Hop

Ron Keeps Hypnotizin' 'Em. Ron "Amen-Ra" Lawrence, who is best known for his work with Sean "Puffy" Combs, the Notorious B.I.G., and LL Cool J, signs a worldwide publishing deal with BMG Songs. Pictured seated, from left, are Combs, producer/artist/Bad Boy Entertainment president; Ron Lawrence; and Ed Woods, Lawrence's attorney. Shown standing, from left, are Clyde Lieberman, VP of East Coast operations at BMG Songs, and Derrick Thompson, VP of urban music at BMG Songs.

Where I'm From: Growing Up Hip Hop

Track Twenty-Eight
<u>Top of My Game</u>

After the year I had, every publishing company wanted to be in business with me. They were throwing all kinds of offers at me to administer my catalog. I ended up striking a deal with BMG. They were an international company with a global presence. I felt that they would provide the greatest exposure for my growing catalog. It was like I had the magic touch. Not only were my songs all over the radio, they were also on huge albums that sold a million copies or more.

    I was running out of space on my wall for my plaques but there was *always* room in my bank account for the money I was getting. I was earning healthy production fees and cashing large publishing checks. Seeds I planted a year ago were bearing fruit a year later. *Money Power* and *Respect* was a number one gold-selling single. It helped give The Lox a *platinum* album. LSG went double platinum. Tyrese went platinum. It was not just about having the right equipment or being lucky.

Where I'm From: Growing Up Hip Hop

My success was attributed to the power of listening. I listened to an entire record from beginning to end. I would turn it up loud and absorb the music. Then I would listen to it at low volume. I needed to know what it would sound like in a club or through headphones. I met with A&R people to get their opinion. There were times I got it right. Other times I had to go back to the lab. I had to listen to what was hot in the streets to determine what the fans would like.

When I used records like Ashford and Simpson's *Street Corner*, Teena Marie's *Behind the Groove* and Cheryl Lynn's *Encore*, I picked them because they had a vibrant sound. It was one thing to attract the listener with a familiar sample, but it was another to add other sounds that either complement or improve upon the original. I might catch a listener the first time with a hot joint from back in the day, but it was another thing to keep them listening repeatedly.

When I constructed my songs, I didn't just make beats, I was creating complete compositions. They had a beginning, middle and end. Take a song like Tyrese's *You Get Yours*. It has a strong bass and drum intro. Throughout the song, the drums have a live feel and remain right in the pocket. I created a bridge and let the drums drop out. Now it is just lead and background vocals for a minute until I bring the mix back in. Some of my songs are not album singles, but they *sounded* like singles.

I was getting pretty good at constructing R&B songs. I could have material, but I needed to have great chemistry with the artist. I remember being exhausted in the studio during the Tyrese project. Tyrese's energy pulled me through. He was hungry and energetic. Tyrese had that fire. I was there at the beginning of his career. It is no accident that he is so successful today.

I had already promised Puff that I would fall back when it came to lifting tracks from the DAT after the Imajin session. I did not know it at the time, but it would happen again when Deric went to the DAT to play songs for Roc-A-Fella Records to hear as they prepared for an upcoming Jay-Z project.

I had created a track featuring a sample of *Let Your Hair Down* by Yvonne Fair. It was a departure from the Bad Boy radio records that I created. My track only consisted of a naked sample with nothing. When Jay-Z heard it, he bought it anyway. Even though the Biz version stuck in mind, I thought I could flip it differently. This was my chance to give it a shot once we recorded the vocals. I booked the session at Quad Recording Studio, the same studio where Tupac was shot a few years before.

Deric & and I arrived early to track the beat in order to have it ready. When Jay and his crew walked in, it was like a comet shot through the studio. Their watches and chains were *gleaming*. I looked at my watch and then I looked at Jay's. Then I looked at mine again. My mind was supposed to be on the session, but I couldn't get past the jewels they were rocking.

Where I'm From: Growing Up Hip Hop

As we sat by side at the mixing board, my curiosity got the best of me. I looked down at his watch. *"So that's white gold, huh?"* He turned his head slowly toward me and said, *"Nah player...it's platinum."* I repeated the word over and over in my head *Platinum*.

The engineer put the sample on repeat while Jay paced back and forth across the room like a LQ chain snatcher looking for his next victim. Finally, he was ready. *"Put the mic on record."* Jay walked in the booth and started spitting his lines. *"I'm from where the hammer's rung, news cameras never come..."*

When he was done, he walked back out of the booth to listen to what he had recorded. He paced back and forth for a few minutes and headed back in the booth for the second line. *"You and your man houndin' every verse in your rhyme where the grams are slung..."* He came back out of the booth and repeated the process. Before long, he was done. There was no paper and pen. There was no rhyme book. Like a Hebrew making bricks without straw, Jay did the unthinkable. Then it hit me. *He's made up these fucking lyrics in his head.* The only other rapper I ever saw do this was Big.

It was like hearing Rakim for the first time all over again. I was witnessing hip hop history in real time. I just saw an emcee rocking platinum jewelry who created an entire song without writing anything down. When Jay's man Sauce Money laid down the hook, the track was perfect.

Where I'm From: Growing Up Hip Hop

A few weeks later, I was back in the studio for a remix session. Besides the engineer and me, Hip Hop, Jay's A&R guy was there for the session too. I used the JV-1080 to dress up the track. It was like I was constructing a sonic skyscraper. Instead of steel or concrete, I used drums, bass, a keyboard sound, bells and whistles to build my structure.

I stayed in the studio all night until the job got done. When it was time to lay the scratches, we tried different DJs for the hook but none of them could get it right. The record company finally called DJ Premier. He was a master at scratching in vocal choruses. Primo came in and knocked it out with ease. We used one of Jay's lines from *Young Gs,* a song he collaborated with Puff on *No Way Out*. We complimented the lyrical theme perfectly. *"Mentally been many places, but I'm Brooklyn's own."* This joint was a departure from what I had been doing in the past. *Where I'm from* flew under the radar for a minute until it resurfaced as one of Jay's most memorable classic songs. I'm proud of the fact hip hop critics have called it the best song in the Hov catalog.

It is funny how you can have everything you want but there is always that one single accomplishment and achievement that makes you feel like you have conquered the world. I have one person who I thank for being a catalyst for that: Faith Evans. She writes, produces and does vocal arrangements. Of course, she's a dope singer. *Vibe* magazine likened her voice to rain----one-minute a "sunshower" and in a split second "an electrical thunderstorm." Faith ground her way to the top. She went from being a studio session singer to becoming a platinum-selling artist. It was good to see her back in the game after the Big situation.

Unlike a lotta female singers, Faith is self-contained. She does not need a producer to hold her hand in the studio. It is the reason why I was shocked when Faith called and invited me to her studio session. She usually preferred to work alone. *"Ron! I'm closing out the album. I need one of those hits. I'm writing to one your tracks, you need to come through!"* Faith was working on her second album. She was on a mission, bouncing back between New York and Atlanta knocking out recording sessions. In New York, Faith had booked time in *three* studios alone. She was serious. When I got to the studio, Faith was bobbing to a heavy bassline. I recognized the track immediately. It was one of the joints from my DAT tape. I had sampled Unlimited Touch's *I Hear Music in the Streets.* I could hear my drum and bass combo injecting the sample with that knock guaranteed to rock the clubs.

When I made the beat, I never intended for it to be an R&B joint but with Faith, I knew it was in good hands. Faith greeted me with a warm smile and a hug. It had a been a while since Trinidad, but we saw each other from time to time. When Faith was house shopping in Jersey, she came out to visit me. I started sitting in on her sessions and we collaborated on a song using one of my other tracks from the DAT tape.

When Faith hit the booth, her voice just floated above the tracks. She did her own backgrounds too. She worked quick. She was a pro. The songs that we worked on----*Love Like This* and *All Night Long* became her signature songs. Faith was known for her ballads. She was like a modern-day torch singer. It was crazy how a couple of up-tempo records would redefine her career. A lot of singers could not pull off being a vocal double threat. I may have made the music, but Faith's writing ability and great sense of melody made those records pop too. It was a rewarding experience because we co-wrote *All Night Long* together. The records would help her *Keep the Faith* album go platinum. *Love Like This* went gold. It was so successful that Bad Boy stopped the single sales of the track in order to push the album. *All Night Long* would establish me as a songwriter. To think it all started with a phone call. *Thanks, Faith.*

Where I'm From: Growing Up Hip Hop

Where I'm From: Growing Up Hip Hop

J-Dub, Boyz II Men and Amen-Ra

Where I'm From: Growing Up Hip Hop

Tyrese Gibson and Amen-RA

Manager Greg Parks, Tyrese and Amen-RA

Where I'm From: Growing Up Hip Hop

Amen-RA and Jay-Z

Where I'm From: Growing Up Hip Hop

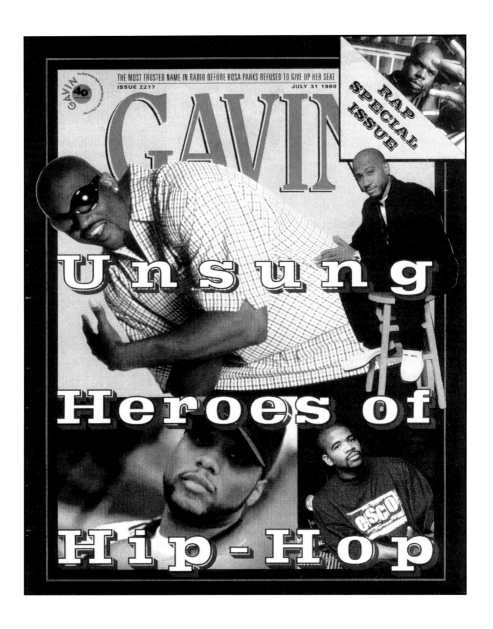

Where I'm From: Growing Up Hip Hop

Where I'm From: Growing Up Hip Hop

✓ Sun Shine

RON "AMEN-RA" LAWRENCE
WORDS BY JOSEPH WILKES
PHOTOGRAPHY BY JAVAD MOORE

It would not be an understatement to say that, as a member of Bad Boy Entertainment's elite Hitmen production squad, Ron "Amen-Ra" Lawrence is responsible for some of the most acclaimed Hip-Hop songs of the mid-to-late '90s.

"I came [to] Bad Boy in like '96, around the time Stevie J., Nasheim [Myrick] and Deric [D-Dot] Angelettie came in," explains Ron. "We all came together like a big assembly line. Everybody played their part."

During that time, the man nicknamed Amen-Ra ("Unseen Force of the Rising Sun" in ancient Egyptian) helmed monster hits like LL Cool J's "Phenomenon" and Jay-Z's "Where I'm From," in addition to Bad Boy classics "Been Around The World" from Puff's *No Way Out* and Biggie's "Hypnotize."

"I started off with a good friend of mine by the name of Herbie Love Bug," says Ron of his early days in Queens. Music was always around him, thanks to his mother who played piano and his father who played guitar. "I didn't know how to use a drum machine. I would sound beats with my mouth." Lawrence's beat-boxing skills quickly led to his first production contribution on Salt N Pepa's hit "I'll Take Your Man."

His abilities would pay off years later at D.C.'s Howard University when he met fellow NY native Sean "Puffy" Combs. Lawrence even credits himself as the first person to take Combs to a recording studio, though their history together didn't give him an edge amongst the in-house competition at Bad Boy.

"Puff always had his favorite Hitmen," Lawrence explains. "I played Mase 'Been Around The World' and Black Rob 'I Love You Baby.' [They] flipped out. Then Puff said, 'I'm taking the records for my album.' And those were tracks he had passed on." But Ron says that once he adapted his sound to what he thought Puff was looking for—mainly funk hits from the '70s—he made the transition to the forefront.

Since leaving the Hitmen fold, Lawrence has maintained a low profile, though he recently produced Beyoncé's lead single from the upcoming film *The Pink Panther*.

"I think New York has lost its sound," says Ron of his return mission. "We need cats to keep that sound alive; that's the foundation of Hip-Hop. I think music should reflect where you come from."

> "I didn't know how to use a drum machine. I would sound beats with my mouth."

DIAMOND D - *STUNTS BLUNTS AND HIP-HOP* (1992)
THIS DIGGIN' IN THE CRATES CREW MEMBER'S CLASSIC DEBUT IS REQUIRED LISTENING FOR THOSE CURIOUS ABOUT THE ART OF SLICING AND DICING OBSCURE BREAKS AND PAIRING THEM WITH WITTY WORDPLAY.

RZA - *ENTER THE WU-TANG: 36 CHAMBERS* (1993)
AS THE ORIGINAL SOUL VOCAL SAMPLER, RZA'S MASTERY OF PRODUCTION OVERSHADOWED HIS RHYME ABILITIES. THE FORMER PRINCE RAKEEM DEBUTED WITH THE SINGLE "WE LOVE YOU RAKEEM" AND THEN "WAS FLOWING LIKE CHRIST" ON THE CLAN'S SEMINAL DEBUT.

Where I'm From: Growing Up Hip Hop

Track Twenty-Nine
<u>Boom Bap and Bamboozled</u>

I was making great R&B records, but I made sure never to stray too far from the hip hop side of the tracks. I scheduled a meeting with Rob "Reef" Tewlow, A&R of Atlantic Records. Rob liked what he heard and picked a track for the Terror Squad, rapper Fat Joe's rap clique. We scheduled a session at Battery Studios in downtown Manhattan. As usual, I got there early to track the song with the engineer. It was studio protocol to have the track ready when an artist showed up for a recording session.

Fat Joe and some of the Terror Squad members showed up except for Big Pun and Cuban Link who were last to arrive. While the crew wrote their verses, I chilled on a love seat by the door watching them write when I heard the elevators door open. The heavy thud of footsteps was approaching fast. Then I heard heavy breathing. Pun staggered into the studio. Fat Joe saw him before I did. He gave me a warning just in the nick of time. *"Yo, need to get up quick, move… MOVE! HE'S GONNA SIT ON YOU!"* As Pun lunged towards me, I jumped up quickly. Pun collapsed on the love seat with a look of relief. He had just missed me. When I played the track, the fellas were amped. My haunting piano and synth sounds gave the track a menacing feel. The bass-heavy circular rhythms were perfect for a hot sixteen. The haze of liquor and weed did little to filter the potency of their rhymes.

Pun set things off first. He had been gaining weight and it was impacting his vocal delivery. He could not flow anymore like he used to. He ended up having to piece his verses together. After the rest of the squad laid their verses, Joe closed the track out with a menacing dialogue. *In for Life* was the first song on Terror Squad's album. Less than six months later, Big Pun died of a heart attack. His career was short, but his impact still endures.

Twenty years after he put me down with the Super Lovers, Hurby was still looking out. He had a small label deal with MCA Records. He was rarely in his office so he would let me use it once a week to take industry meetings. I was an independent producer for hire, but it looked good to have a corporate space to handle business.

I took a meeting with my man Steve Jackson. He was a high school principal in Bayside, Queens. Steve was a talent scout of sorts. He would find local talent at Bayside High and bring them to me for auditions. When he showed up for the meeting, he brought a young female singer with him. She was about to graduate from high school. Her name was Olivia Longott. She was very attractive. When she sang for me in the office, I was impressed. I told Steve I was ready to take her into the studio to cut demos for her. We booked studio time at Hurby's to cut some tunes. He had built a studio in his mothers garage. Steve and I could not come to a proper agreement and the deal fell through, but I knew Olivia would not have to wait long for her shot.

"Rakim's coming out with a new album and he needs some fire." I was at the Universal offices when Dino Delvaille told me Ra was working on a new joint. Dino was A&Ring the project. He laid out an unorthodox creative blueprint for me to follow. Rakim lived out in Connecticut and he did not like traveling to the city. I would have to record the tracks in Manhattan and give them to Universal who would deliver the masters to Rakim by messenger. He would record his vocals at home and send them back when he was done. I did two tracks with my boy Vic, *Uplift* and *Real Shit*.

When I heard the completed tracks, I looked at the speaker and did a doubletake. *Rakim was singing the hook.* It was dope as shit! I wish the public could have heard it. It would have been the equivalent of watching an outtake of Jay-Z dancing in a music video. Ra didn't want to release this version of *Real Shit*. *"Yo Gee, you know I don't sing right?"* *"I can't release the song like that Gee, I'm not a singer".* I tried to convince him. *"This could be something dope"* Just like he held the mic tight like a grudge, Ra stood firm on his decision and would not budge. His delivery was so fly that when we tried different artists on the hook, nobody matched Ra's performance, so we scrapped them. Rakim had a good relationship with Canibus. We put him on the song and gave it a new chorus. It didn't work. Ra called me back. *"Take 'em off Gee, it's not gon' work."* He felt the Canibus's direction was different from the concept he created.

Rakim ended up doing the chorus himself and changing the words, I could only imagine how that song would have come out with Ra singing the original hook!

If anyone told me during my emcee days back in Queens, that industry doors would embrace me as a producer, I would have called them crazy. If they told me I would be working in the film industry, I *would not* put any stock in that prediction. That is what happened when Bill Stephney called me and told me that Spike Lee was working on a movie called *Bamboozled* and I would be a great fit. Spike needed a hip-hop score for the film. I took Bill at his word because I knew his resume. Bill was instrumental in Public Enemy's success back in the Eighties. He had done college radio. He was a writer, musician and producer. He did marketing and promotions. He owned a record label. Now Bill was running his own entertainment company.

We met in Bill's office and I played the tracks for Spike. He was impressed with my music and we exchanged phone numbers. After the meeting, Spike tried to wave down a cab. I offered to give him a ride to his destination. As we talked in the car, we hit it off. Spike graciously answered all my questions about his films.

Where I'm From: Growing Up Hip Hop

Spike called me the next day and we discussed the film details. I also asked him for a part in the movie. He politely declined and told me that all the roles were cast but he could possibly fit me in somewhere.

A week or so later, I met some of Spike's cast members. The actors slotted to play his fictional Mau Mau rap group were there. Most of them were hip hop people like Mos Def, Charli Baltimore, MC Search, DJ Scratch and Canibus. Actor Gano Grills and the spoken word poet/actor Mums rounded out the crew.

The track that Spike chose for the group had a dark and sinister feel to it. The group hated it. Spike stuck to his guns and set up a session at D&D Studios in Manhattan. We sat around the mixing board vibin' off each other and then Mos Def came up with a hook for the track. *"Who the crew? M-A-U, M-A-U, gun ready/bout to attack the track with BLAK IZ BLAK/well how black? BLAK HEART, BLAK MIND, BLAK SOUL/Mau Maus (LEE-LEE LEE!) We was born to roll/who the crew? M-A-U, M-A-U, aim fire/bout to attack the track when BLAK IZ BLAK/how black? BLAK WOMB TIL WE REACH THE BLACK HEARSE/what's black? - SHADE OF THE UNIVERSE"*

We flipped out when we heard the chorus. Everybody started knocking out their lyrics. Now it was time to record. Since Mums was a gifted poet, I had him do the intro.

Canibus was slotted to be the first to rhyme but he wasn't with it. *"Naah, B. I ain't feelin' that."* He stayed in competition mode. The way Canibus and Mos Def were bumping heads it caused friction, draining all the energy out of the room.

In the end, Mos Def decided to do it. The session ended up being pretty good. The vocals captured the essence of the Mau Mau's film scenes. Spike was very happy with the outcome.

After the session, I dropped in on him during the film's editing process. I rode the elevator to an upper floor and walked into a huge room. The layout was amazing. There was editing equipment up in the balcony. A huge screen was in the center of the room. The layout was set up like an actual theater. The room must have been used for private screenings prior to actual film releases. It was exciting to see all the moving parts of this film process. I wanted to learn how it all worked.

"Hey Ron, I have bad news, your screen credit was omitted." Spike's music supervisor called. He did not beat around the bush. He never gave me an explanation either. I needed a logical reason why credit for my hard work was not going to make it to the silver screen. I tried to rationalize it in my head. Spike's main music guy was Terence Blanchard. *Maybe my credit next to his would look out of place. He's a classical-jazz guy and I am hip hop.* I racked my brain trying to figure things out, but it just did not make any sense.

Where I'm From: Growing Up Hip Hop

I called Spike and pleaded my case. *"I was compensated, but credit is much more important to me. If it's too late to fix it, can you look out for me on your future projects?"* He promised he would. True to Spike's word, a year or so later he called with job offers. He had a Mountain Dew and Pepsi commercial lined up that he wanted me to score.

I jumped at the chance. The job paid well, I would gain more film scoring experience and there was a chance I would get to work with Beyoncé who was on her way to becoming a mega-star. She had just wrapped up her first acting role in a hip-hop update of the classic *Carmen Jones* musical. Beyoncé played the original Dorothy Dandridge lead.

Spike filmed a commercial with Beyoncé in her movie wardrobe attire singing the *Dat'sLove/Habanera* classical piece from the original film. There were about 100 instruments on the song. Spike wanted me to add a hip-hop edge to the tracks. Beyoncé also wanted to do some of her vocals over to improve the notes. The plan was to meet her at a studio in South Beach to complete the project.

I flew out during a snow storm and the temperature was zero. When I walked into Newark Liberty International Airport, I wore a big-ass heavy coat. When I left Miami International, I was stripping down. It was eighty degrees. I was loving it. Instantly, I knew one day, I would move here. As usual, I got to the studio early. Beyoncé entered from a back alley to avoid crowds. We exchanged greetings and got to work.

Beyoncé was a consummate professional. She fixed her notes and knocked them out in one take. Beyoncé worked so quickly that I was able to fly back to Jersey the same day. It was still freezing when I got back. It was amazing how in sixteen hours I experienced extreme weather changes all in a single day.

The other job didn't go so well. Spike sent me the video of the Mountain Dew commercial with a simple code used to sync audio sounds to film.

I finished the job and sent it back. The next day I got a call. It was Spike. He was on speaker and the rest of his staff was in the room. He was pissed. The edge in his nasal bark was unmistakable. *"Ron, why did you remove the simpte code from the video?"* I closed my eyes and shook my head. *I felt like I just missed a layup at the Garden.* While I was synching the video to a beat that I had in my Pro Tools software, I accidentally deleted the simpte code. I had forgotten to add the code back in.

I apologized but Spike was not having it. *"Without that simpte code I'm gonna have problems syncing up the beat to the master edit of the video!"* Then all I heard was silence. It felt like a repeat of the LL fiasco at the Hit Factory. After that incident I never worked with Spike again.

Where I'm From: Growing Up Hip Hop

Clive Davis was a chameleon. It was like he had nine lives. In the early Seventies, he guided CBS to a record two billion dollars in annual sales. When fiscal mismanagement and payola charges got him booted from CBS, he created his own label, Arista Records that he ran for nearly thirty years. After being forced to step down from Arista due to age restrictions, Clive launched J Records and in true Clive fashion, he was looking for hits. He was still in the game at sixty-eight.

His label was just a week old when my manager Fran Spero called. *"Guess what Ron, Clive Davis wants to meet you."* My tracks record at Bad Boy preceded me. In '97 Bad Boy delivered three multi-platinum albums and a slew of platinum singles to Arista. Three years later, we were still putting out hits.

Now, I was at Clive's office in the historic luxury Waldorf-Astoria hotel listening to him play music from some of his new signees. His voice was friendly and warm. In his inviting Brooklyn timbre, Clive laid out a game plan like Phil Jackson running a play to get the ball to Jordan with five seconds left in the game. I was MJ. *"I just signed Alicia Keys, Olivia, Jimmy Cozier and Luther Vandross, Ron. You have free range to work with any of these artists if you chose. Just come back with hit records and we can make some deals happen. Let's start with Jimmy Cozier first".* I was having a déjà vu' moment. It was like hearing Puff lay out his master plan to attack radio four years earlier. Here I was again---on the ground floor---about to be part of something big.

When Clive requested that I use *Cold, Cold World*, a song that I worked on with my man Mark Batson recorded by Bad Boy artist Carl Thomas, the magnitude of his power sunk in. He was able to override the standard contractual window to use a song that was associated with his *old* label. Now we were negotiating a new deal to re-record a track my man Mark and I produced a year ago for Carl on a *new* artist. That was power. I was ready to go. I had history with Alicia and Olivia. I had worked with them back when they were teenagers. I was anxious to work with Luther.

Amen-Ra and Spike Lee

Track Thirty
Luther

I decided to hire my sister Bernie as my attorney. After finishing up law school at Howard, she wanted to work as an entertainment lawyer. I decided to give her a shot negotiating my Luther Vandross production contract. This was not an easy deal. I threw Bernie out there into the big leagues right out the gate. She knew that she could not mess it up. Jimmy Cozier's track was already done, so I was looking ahead.

After I left our meeting at the Waldorf, I went straight to work. I used my MPC-300 to create a percolating drum pattern. I created guitar and bass sounds with the ASR-10 module and pulled other sounds from the JV2080. After my success with Faith, I wanted to recreate the magic with another female writer. Instead of looking for a seasoned songwriter, I hooked up with Brooke Richardson She knocked it out of the park. She wrote a great lyric with a catchy storyline about a lover who was ready to move on from a relationship but did not know how to end it for good. Once the song was completed, I gave it to my manager.

A week later I received a phone call from J Records, while I was on interstate 280 headed home. Luther Vandross loved the song and would call me soon. I was so excited, that I almost crashed my 740 IL. I had to coach Bernie on the deal, but she ended up doing such a good job, I started passing on my other contracts for her to negotiate. She was knocking them out left and right. It felt good to have her close by.

I wouldn't have to schedule appointments in advance like I would have to do with my other attorneys. Bernie ended up launching her own firm and nearly twenty years later, she is doing great work with rapper 21 Savage and producers Bangladesh and Tay Keith.

When Luther called me to book studio time for December, he told me how much he loved the record and looked forward to working with me. That said a lot since Luther usually worked with his own team. I was equally impressed and surprised at how he managed his schedule. He booked me months in advance.

Luther was a master at making Quiet Storm ballads, but I was a fan of his up-tempo joints like *Searchin', Glow of Love* and *Never Too Much.* I wanted to take him there. When I walked into the Hit Factory, I was in for a rude awakening. *"Ron, I liked the track but no offense, I don't allow producers involved in my sessions while the song is being recorded."* I was crushed. The rumors were true. Luther *was* a diva. All those En Vogue and Anita Baker beefs *were* true. I would have loved to be a fly on the wall if he would have told a control freak like Puff that *he* had to leave. I didn't object. This man had ten consecutive platinum and multiplatinum studio albums in seventeen years. *If it ain't broke, don't fix it.* By this time, most studios had already switched over to Pro Tools. I already recorded the session on a CD. I handed it over to the engineer and bounced. It wouldn't be my first encounter with Luther over the creative direction.

    Luther called me back in a few days. Soon, he felt comfortable enough to let me hang out in the studio. He made sure to remind me that this wasn't normal protocol. *"Ron, I normally don't do this. You're the first."* Together, we produced the vocals. When he called me back to hear the finished product, I didn't like it. *"We need to do the lead vocal over."* Luther rolled his eyes. He did not reply but his face said it all. *Who are YOU to tell me how to sing?* I stood my ground. We both compromised a little to get things done.

    One battle I did not win was how to record background vocals. My generation of producers were studio rats. We had no problem staying in the studio all night stacking vocals. Luther was from a different era where musicians and singers recorded together. Singers rehearsed the song and got it down *before* they hit the booth. They recorded together and sang in different harmonies. These singers had it down to a science, bouncing around the city doing multiple sessions in the time it took guys from my era to complete one session. They were so efficient, they picked up a lot of checks that way. Why stay four hours in the studio when you could knock things out in two?

Luther's methods threw me off for a minute. Before he started making his own records, he made a great living as a background singer. Luther sang with everyone from David Bowie to Roberta Flack to Chic. He did countless jingles for TV and radio. He had won awards for his behind the scenes contributions and negotiated his own financial terms charging top dollar. He owned an elegant apartment in Midtown. He financed his own recording sessions without the help of a record label. Before the entire world even knew he was, Luther was already a star in the industry.

When he finally signed with CBS Records, he demanded and received complete creative control. Luther had a crew of background singers he always worked within the studio. When I heard them sing, I understood how he sold so many records for so long. I watched Kevin Owens, Brenda White-King, Cindy Mizelle, Robin Clark, Cissy Houston, Tawatha Agee and Fonzi Thornton go in the booth and work their magic on *How Do I Tell Her*. It was like watching a concert in the studio. Their vocals were in different harmony and all on key, giving the record a natural and organic feel.

It was like listening to four lead singers at the same time or hearing a Grandmaster Flash and the Furious Five routine where "five emcees sounded like one."

Where I'm From: Growing Up Hip Hop

I pulled in the engineer all-star from my Bad Boy days, Prince Charles Alexander to mix the song and brought in Fred Cash on bass and Ira Seigel & Ricky Kenyarnz on guitars. They did an excellent job. *How Do I Tell Her* was not a single but people loved it---especially the signature background vocals too (yeah, you were right, Luther).

The session meant a lot to me because I also got to bond with Luther. He had just moved back to New York from Cali. He was back in his Manhattan Brownstone that he kept in the city. In between sessions, I shared with him how much I loved Cissy Houston's background vocals on Paul Simon's *Mother and Child Reunion* thirty years ago. Luther was shocked. He did a double take. *"What do you know about that?"* I smiled. I told him that it was a popular record in Dominica. It broke the ice between us. He gave me his number and every now and then, we would talk from time to time. Luther was a private person. For him to be comfortable enough, opening up was something special.

My biggest regret is that I do not have photos of the sessions. I did not load my camera properly and missed out. Luther's album sold a million copies in less than six months.

His single *Take You Out* was a hit. Everybody loved that hook. It would turn up as the chorus of a Jay-Z song a couple of years later. The record I produced for him got a lot of praise as well. Luther's comeback was a platinum success, but he was after something that had eluded him his entire career.

Luther wanted a number one pop record. He would achieve that dream on his next album, *Dance with My Father*. It would be his last. While in the process of finishing the record, Luther had a stroke at home. He was alone for seven hours before he was found. He died a couple of years later. Luther left a void in the industry that has yet to be filled.

Chapter Thirty-One
<u>Changes</u>

Whenever I was digging for beats, I always seemed to come across Donald Byrd's *Spaces and Places* album. It is a great record. A go-to joint that many rap producers used to make some dope records. It is a great one to zone out to. *Changes* was my favorite song on the album. The brassy horns and drum shuffle always transported me back to the days when I went to the West Indian Day carnivals in Brooklyn where the Caribbean rhythms never failed to stir my soul.

If my life was a photograph, *Change's* lyrics provided the perfect caption. It summarized everything I had to do to get to this point. I had worked with some legendary artists. I had made great music. I felt my place in hip hop history was sealed. I wanted to continue to make music, but I wanted to express myself in other creative ways.

My contract with Bad Boy expired and I had no desire to renew it. I just walked away. I had had a great run with a great crew, but it was time to move on. Deric and I also ended our partnership. We had a couple falling outs that led to us not speaking for some time.

We eventually patched things up later, but for now our separation was for the best.

I sensed the music game changing. It was time to diversify and broaden my horizons My experience with Spike in the world of movie-making left an impression on me. I wanted to study filmmaking in the future. For now, it was about continuing to solidify my foundation and keep striking while the iron was hot.

I also took my personal life to the next level. Shay and I got married. We had been together nearly five years at this point. I wanted to settle down with a family by the time I was thirty-five. Time was ticking. On June 17, 2000 we said our vows in front of over a hundred of our family and close friends at a resort in the Catskills. Love was in the air that day. Being married was just the icing on the cake. As far as I was concerned Shay, her daughter Shayla and I were already family.

The next day, we were off to the Caribbean for a seven-day honeymoon cruise. As we walked together on the beach, we discussed our future. We both wanted children. The energy of the music business was shifting to Atlanta, so it made sense for us to consider making a move down south. As we laid out our life goals and plotted our strategy, the breezy tropical air carried our words out to an awaiting universe.

Where I'm From: Growing Up Hip Hop

Black Rob's album was platinum. Mase's second album was gold. Bad Boy also had another dope rapper on deck named G. Dep. I would also produce a single on his album called *Everyday*. Things were looking good. My phone stayed ringing. One day, I received a call from a guy from the old neighborhood. It was Kwamé calling looking for help. He was looking to get back into the game. From the late Eighties until the early Nineties, Kwamé had made some great records, but now, things had really slowed down for him. Rap music had changed in the past decade and he was out of the mix. He wanted me to manage him.

I wasn't too crazy about the idea. I had my hands full. I had a lot of projects on my plate. Kwamé was tied to an earlier era. Unfortunately, the industry could be cruel to classic rap artists and producers on the comeback trail. They were considered washed up. Relics of the past. It didn't help that some of Big's lyrics put a nail in Kwamé's career coffin, turning rap fans against him. Managing acts was a full-time job.

I reconsidered. The first thing I had to do was rebrand Kwamé. I had an idea. *"If you wanna start over, you need to change your name."* From that point on, Kwamé became K-1 Million and things started picking up. My plan worked. I had gotten him on a few projects, including a placement for the soundtrack of a hit movie. Kwamé was back in the game. He got a new apartment and a brand-new car. I felt good about being able to reach back out to the hood and help people who I came up with. Most of the time, I had a lot of great experiences as a producer but sometimes things did not go as smoothly. Once, I was hired to produce a solo record for a Nicci Gilbert, the former lead singer of nineties female R&B trio Brownstone. Nicci was a great vocalist who sang with a dramatic flair. She had great range. I had an idea to add some live violins to her music. I needed to hire some session players to provide the strings.

When I showed up to work, the A&R guy canceled the session without telling me, plus he didn't want to spend money on violin players. I was pissed for a couple reasons. I had to come into the city for nothing and I felt my creative ideas were not being respected. I walked out of Unique Studios steaming.

I was on Broadway and Fifty-Fourth headed for my car when I ran into a check. An A&R working with Mary J. Blige pulled me into the project just like that. *"Yo homie, we working on Mary J's album right now, you got some heat?"* My DAT tape was like American Express. I never left home without it. *"No doubt. I got something."* I followed him to the studio. Mary was there and I played her my tracks.

My timing was perfect. The track I submitted would close out her album budget. She did the vocals and scheduled me to come in for the final mix in a few days. When it was done, I got a call from Mary and from the tone in her voice, she was not pleased. She did not like the mix. *"I can't hear my vocals! The mix is too loud! You need *to fix it, Ron!"* I hopped in my 740 IL and jumped on the turnpike. I walked in the studio expecting to be on the end of another LL-type tirade. The chilly reception I got was even worse. Mary and her then-husband Kendu looked disgusted.

Mary barely spoke to me. After that experience, I thought to myself, *all money ain't good money.* I changed my mind when Mary's *No More Drama* dropped. The album sold almost a couple million the first time out. When they put out a special edition version the record sold another million copies. It was big around the world too. All in all, the record moved around six million units worldwide.

There is a rule that we have in the industry. *Don't count the money until the check clears.* It would be a while before I would get paid. I got some bad news from Bernie. *"Ronald, you're being sued."* I had walked Bernie through the entertainment game and now my little sister was my lawyer. I was glad, considering the situation I found myself in.

Mary's brother Bruce had written lyrics to the track I produced for Mary. The album blew up and I guess Bruce's ex-girlfriend saw dollar signs. She claimed that it was *her* lyrics that Bruce used, and she was suing for 100% of the copyright. I had nothing to do with the situation, but I got dragged into the lawsuit. I had to pay a bunch of legal fees to fight her allegations.

I was rarely involved in situations like these. Legal hassles messed with my creativity. A lot of the songs that I had worked on in the past were sample heavy and needed clearances from the copyright owners. If the sample-clearing process took too long, publishing royalties could be delayed. When things like that happened, it affected my concentration and I suffered from producer's block. I was in Manhattan when I bumped into an A&R who offered me a spot-on LL's new project.

LL was recording his tenth album on Def Jam Records. He had been in the game now for nearly twenty years and had outlasted everybody he came up with. He was still making hits. Since we last hooked up at the Hit Factory, LL had made a complete physical transformation. It was like he had turned back the clock. LL was lean and muscular. He was eating clean. When he told me that he ran twenty miles at 6:30 in the morning, I could see why he had so much energy. It was like he was training for a heavyweight bout instead of making a new album. Five years ago, I was a hired gun on a hot streak. This time things were different. LL made it clear that he was looking to me to provide direction. Most producers were intimidated by him and let him do his thing. He made it clear that he needed guidance to make the best record possible.

We worked on a song for his album that he called *10*. It had a simple name, but it spoke volumes. LL was ten albums deep in a long career that was a couple decades in the making. The record was another platinum banger for him.

After the session we reminisced about the old days back in Queens. When I did the old routine, he rocked with his crew thirty years ago, he burst out in his signature laugh that sounded like it rained down from a mountaintop. Things with LL worked out so well, he flew me out to LA to work on a children's book with him. While I was out in Cali, I received an invitation to meet with New Heights Entertainment, an emerging company providing customized services for their roster of songwriters, producers and artists.

I did not know too much about the company. When I got to Hollywood, I recognized the New Heights building from back in the days when I was hustling up producer jobs around the city during the Shai days. The building had strong historical ties to the entertainment world. Actor Charlie Chaplin owned it first. Years later, it became a studio complex that belonged to Muppets creator Jim Henson. A&M Records had a recording studio there too. I met with New Heights CEO Alan Melina and played my tracks. Soon the meeting took a different turn.

"Who are you with, Ron? Who's handling your business?" I told Alan I was a free agent, but I was looking for new management. He said he was interested in managing me. By the time I finished LL's book project, Alan had reached out and submitted an offer. I took it. Alan and New Heights got to work immediately. They fixed my

publishing nightmare with BMG. I recouped on my earlier admin deal and entered into a co-publishing agreement that netted me a nice upfront advance.

It was a good move. The music industry was downsizing. Labels were starting to pull back on huge advances and large recording budgets. The days of the big producer checks were coming to an end. When things dried up, I wanted to be ready. I was aligned with a global publishing company and a Hollywood entertainment firm who redirect my music to new revenue-generating opportunities.

Where I'm From: Growing Up Hip Hop

Val Anthony, me and Deston Ausar

SIDE IV

Survivor (2003-Infinity)

Track Thirty-Two
Lights, Camera, Action

Working with Spike gave me access me to the film world. I hoped my deal with New Heights would continue to do the same. Having a West Coast-based company could help me get more work. I wanted to keep scoring films and commercials. I wanted my songs in movies and on TV. Thanks to Derickson's coaching back in Queens, I still had a great eye and my camera skills were on point. I was thinking of producing or directing films.

On January 21, 2003, my goals were slowly shaping up to be a reality. It was the day Val, my first-born son was born. I documented his every move. I took pictures and videotaped little Val every chance I got. I even edited the content and turned them into a video. I showed them to my good friend Lynn Dow. She always supported my work. *"This is great! You know you have a great eye. Have you ever thought of enrolling in film school?"*

Lynn convinced me to enroll at the New York Film Academy. The next thing you know I was back in the classroom. I took notes and soaked up everything. I studied the way apertures worked and how they impacted film lighting. I learned to manipulate shutter speeds and distinguish between ISO conversions. I soaked up every technical component that was critical to making films. I spent hours in bookstores devouring books to stay ahead of my class. I was a master in the art of knowledge transfer. I studied architecture in school, so I understood all the moving parts that led to creating films. Through my producer skills I learned project management, so I understood budgets and how to deal with creative and technical roadblocks that came with working on projects.

I was a hands-on cat, so I was not intimidated by the equipment we used in class. My experience in using Pro Tools allowed me to add sounds to my visual work. It gave me an edge over everyone else. I had all areas covered but my instructor did not want to give me credit. She didn't believe I was an amateur like everyone else.

During our class encounters, her tone was always condescending and judgmental. *"Have you worked in the film industry before? It seems like you've done this before."* She refused to acknowledge I was just a gifted student who was in his element. She seemed to think I was cheating.

Our final project was to shoot a black and white silent film. I took it a step further. I shot a color film with sound. It was a process we were exposed to only from a theory perspective. We only studied definitions and technical terms. There were no hands-on or application-based instructional demonstrations to prepare us for the actual work I was doing. On presentation day, my joint stood out. It had voiceovers, and sound effects, the whole nine. I synced up everything with Pro Tools. I didn't just have a class project. I had a *real* industry joint. I looked into the disapproving eyes of some of my classmates. *I could tell they were hating.*

Where I'm From: Growing Up Hip Hop

Chapter Thirty-Three
<u>Strictly Business</u>

My first meeting with New Heights landed me a management deal and a new publishing situation. My second meeting would also put me on the path to work with another music legend. My new manager Alan Malina came to West Orange to hear a track I was working on. We went down to my basement studio. I pushed play and the sound of strings filled the room. A light shower of tinkling keys kicked off a breezy midtempo track that was tailor-made for radio.

Alan liked it. He passed it along to Kawan (KP) Prather, executive A&R for Arista Records. KP wanted to record the track for his artist Sara Divine. Alan sent over a team of writers to my house: Aleese Simmons, Katrina Willis, Philip "Silky" White. Things went great. Sara recorded the song. They called it *Wonderful*. Sara left with the demo but after a few months had gone by, Alan learned that the album was on hold indefinitely. He started shopping *Wonderful* to other labels. As the song made its rounds around the industry, it reached the ears of LA Reid. That was a good sign. LA started out as a songwriter himself. He owned his own label and now he was running Arista Records. Just like his predecessor Clive Davis, LA wasted no time getting down to business. *"Ron, this song is great. I would like to give it to Aretha Franklin. We're looking for material for her new album."* LA also offered me a ten-song deal with Arista.

Once again, Bernie handled the negotiations. She did a great job, and everything went smooth. Because Aretha didn't fly, I flew out to Detroit to work on the project at her palatial home in Bloomfield Hills. Aretha had a reputation around the industry for being very strong-willed.

We had two different styles of working. I wanted Aretha's vocals to stay consistent with the melodies already on the demo I produced. Aretha wanted to sing the melodies the way she heard them in her head. The session got a little tense. I could tell she was reluctant to take my direction in terms of how she was supposed to sing. It had long been her domain.

Looking back at the session, it must have been a bit of a challenge for Aretha to adapt to the younger generation's way of creating music. She was used to having more input in the creative process. In an interview she stated that when she wrote and produced the music it ensured listeners would "get more of her" compared to "three or four people working on a song."

I respected Aretha's musical pedigree and admired her accomplishments, but I had to make sure her vocals were perfect.

Confronting her or being overly critical could shut her down. I had an idea. *"Let's go back to the demo and listen to the reference vocal and we'll take it from there."* After Aretha heard the melody, it finally sunk in. she went back and re-recorded multiple parts of her lead vocal. It was perfect. I used them as finishing vocals in the mix. Things went smoothly after that.

The song we worked on---*Wonderful*---was the first single from her *So Damn Happy* album. It went on to win a Grammy Award for Best Traditional R&B performance. It was a major accomplishment for Aretha. It extended her streak of having a hit record in every decade going back to the sixties.

Wonderful's success proved a classic artist could make contemporary music. It allowed LA Reid to put his stamp on Arista by delivering a hit for the label's flagship artist. The song's success boosted my resume and proved that I could deliver hits across various artists and genres.

In 2005, my manager Alan flew songwriter Charmelle Cofield out to Jersey to work with me. We came up with a great song called *A Woman Like Me.* As the song was being shopped, I got a call from Gee Roberson. Gee was a music executive who worked with everyone from Jay-Z to Kanye West. He heard our song and wanted it for R&B singer Sunshine Anderson. She had a big hit with *Heard It All Before* a few years ago.

Where I'm From: Growing Up Hip Hop

We struck a deal, but it fell apart, due to Sunshine experiencing complications with her label, Atlantic Records. Her album would be on hold for a year.

A while later, I got a call from my manager Alan. He had great news. *"Beyoncé has the demo and is going to use it for the Pink Panther movie."* Beyoncé had landed a role as a singer in the film and was looking for material. According to industry protocol, since I never signed a producer declaration with Atlantic Records to work with Sunshine Anderson, I would be able to walk away with the song and offer it to Beyoncé.

There was one problem. If I wanted our song to be featured in the movie, I would have to give up all the publishing rights. I rejected the offer. *"There's no way I'm giving up my publishing. If they're still interested, I want forty-thousand up front and all my publishing rights."* At this point in my career, I had worked with so many established artists that I felt that the Beyoncé deal wouldn't make or break me. Three days later, I received a counteroffer. Since the song was already written into the movie, it was hard to kill the deal. I received a request to allow Beyoncé to change a few lines for ten percent of the publishing rights. It required that Charmelle and I both would give up five percent to Beyoncé. I approved the deal and we moved forward.

The song was added to the *Pink Panther's* project. The movie was a global success. For once, it felt good to dictate the terms instead of going along to get along.

I never forgot about how much I enjoyed Florida. After a huge snowstorm hit the East Coast in 2005, I was ready to sell my home and make the move to Florida. That summer, Shay and I flew to Orlando to look around.

We didn't find anything we liked. We came back to Jersey disappointed over the limited prospects. We decided to give it another try. We flew down to Palm Beach County to check out Wellington, a small town that came highly recommended by a few friends. We fell in love with the area and put a down payment to build a new home. The house wouldn't be ready until the first week of the new year. Shay was pregnant again so there was no rush.

In November my second son Deston Ausar Lawrence was born. The timing was perfect. We welcomed the new addition to our family and looked forward to a fresh start in a new place. When we put the house in West Orange up for sale, it sold immediately. Six months after we arrived in Wellington, my in-laws moved down and bought their home five houses away from us.

Our new home was quiet and serene. There were palm trees everywhere. I felt like I was on some retirement shit. For a minute I thought I made a rash move that would take me out of the New York mix. Maybe I had left too soon.

    I erased the lingering second thoughts from my mind. I was here and wanted to make the best of it. It was time to start focusing on my family and Shayla, Val, and Deston.

    I started to invest in real estate. I bought another house in Florida and owned another in Alpharetta, Georgia. Things were looking good. I recouped my publishing advance from BMG. From this point forward all my publishing royalties would go straight to my bank account. BMG didn't want me to go. I paid them ten stacks upfront to leave my deal. I was a free agent.

    I was settling into my new life. I was enjoying the much slower pace. I loved my neighborhood. It had all the great amenities I could ever want. Supermarkets, movie theaters, malls and just about anything I needed was right around me. I even had great neighbors. I never had to really leave the area for anything. My life was good growing up, but I wanted something different for my kids. I wanted them to have a better life than I did. Watching Val and Deston grow up right before my eyes was one of the greatest gifts God has ever given me.

Where I'm From: Growing Up Hip Hop

Charles Goldstuck, Amen-RA, Clive Davis and Alan Malina (Manager)

Amen-Ra and Aretha Franklin

Where I'm From: Growing Up Hip Hop

To NARAS and the Voting Academy
It is always a tremendous thrill and acknowledgement to receive a Grammy

Many thanks to Joey Arbagey, Vice President A&R, Arista Records

Ron Lawrence, Producer and Writer

Writers: Philip "Silky" White, Katrina Willis and Aleese Simmons

You all are so "Wonderful"

Love Ya Always, Aretha

Chapter Thirty-Four
Cipher Complete

My man Sonny and I were on the phone chopping it up. We were reminiscing on childhood memories and great times we had hanging out at 127 Park. I was about eleven when I met Sonny. Later, when he converted to Islam, he started calling himself Hassan. I remember when Hassan and his friends would come and hang out on my block. They were attracted to my older sisters so I would see them around often.

Hassan and his crew were the first ones from our neighborhood to go to Disco Fever. After soaking up the hip-hop vibe, they would bring back the latest dance steps to the hood. Hassan was also a Golden Gloves boxer. When Eric B would go on the road, Hassan and the Paid in Full posse always held him down. During his early days, Eric B had a lot of heart but he would always get himself into situations that he couldn't handle. If Hassan was around, he would get him out of trouble.

During our conversations, we often discussed why East Elmhurst never came up in hip hop history discussions. They were always left out. Then a lightbulb went off in our heads. *Why not make a documentary about our neighborhood?* During our research and brainstorming sessions, we realized The Hurst documentary would be incomplete without Brooklyn, Harlem and the entire Queens in the mix. Shining light on those early DJs and exploring their contributions in building the hip-hop pyramid would make the cipher complete.

No one had ever focused on the other boroughs. We would be the first. We located all the heavy hitters. Pete DJ Jones and the Disco Twins. We tracked down DJ Lance and people from DJ Flowers' crew. We found Infinity Machine, Baby J and King Charles. My friend Lucio Dutch put me in touch with DJ Hollywood and I reached out to my brother Dony. Hassan hired a cameraman.

That summer we started filming. Our interview subjects were amazing. When we put the camera in their faces, they gave up stories that were fresh, wild, fly and bold. They reminisced on the equipment they used. The parties they rocked and music they played. The provided insight about the fashion. It was important to make a film that broke down hip hop's regional textures the way R&B and jazz were.

When making *Founding Fathers*, we weren't trying to follow the Bronx attitude when recounting the story of hip hop's origins. Our interview subjects did not tear anybody down to build themselves up.

They just added a fresh narrative to a story that had grown stale with time.

Hassan and I mined the fertile soil of the Hurst and surrounding areas and extracted a precious jewel. We considered hiring an intern to edit the film. Instead, I decided to put the skills I learned in school and working with Spike to good use and give it a shot. Hassan and I went back and forth during the editing process.

As we refined our precious gem, we knew it needed weight and clarity, so Hassan reached out to Chuck D from Public Enemy to narrate the film. Chuck's powerful commentary gave it the polish that we needed to put it over the top.

Our diamond was far from being conflict-free. Over a decade after we put *Founding Fathers* together, it still sparks arguments and debates surrounding hip hop history. *To think it all started with a gem of an idea.*

Where I'm From: Growing Up Hip Hop

Hassan Pore and Ron Lawrence at NYI Film Festival, 2010

Where I'm From: Growing Up Hip Hop

Chapter Thirty-Five
Standing Strong and Staying Afloat

In January 2012, Moms took her last breath. My brother called me with the news. After having a stroke, she was admitted to the hospital and went into cardiac arrest. Her health had been poor for a while. Over the past few years she had a series of seizures and strokes. These physical setbacks required her to spend long periods of time in the hospital until she was well enough to go to rehab to learn to walk again.

This last stroke had really taken a toll on her. She had a habit of forgetting to take her blood pressure medication and things caught up with her. During my last visit, she seemed fine, but the after-effects of the stroke had taken away her short-term memory. It was hard accepting the severity of her condition.

Moms was a true renaissance woman. She was the creative soul who made her own wardrobe. Moms was a teacher and academic mentor---a shaper of young minds. She was a successful graduate student and a mathematical genius. She was a refined woman with a rich taste for the classics. When she played the piano, intricate Mozart concertos sprung effortlessly from her fingertips. The depths of her abundance of love was endless. It was always more than an enough to go around for her huge family. Spending time and talking to her I knew her memory would not be the same.

Not long after, she was diagnosed with cancer. Doctors felt she was too old for any type of chemotherapy. She had the operation and recovered well, but in the end her health issues took their toll. Mom was 82 years old when she passed away. The whole family flew back to East Elmhurst for her funeral. She was laid to rest at Flushing Cemetery in Queens. *I'll Always Love My Mama* will forever evoke wonderful memories of Moms.

After receiving my cancer diagnosis, it was time to get things moving. After seeing another doctor who specialized in removing tumors. I took a few more tests and then it was official. I was diagnosed with the early stage 3 colorectal cancer. My colon though was not the problem. There was a tumor in my upper rectum, that was the problem. Because the rectum is attached to the colon, a diagnosis of either colorectal or rectal cancer is possible. Tumors must be removed as soon as possible prior to any operation.

This meant I would have to undergo radiation to shrink the tumor. I went to see a radiologist who scheduled me for twenty-eight days of radiation. I would have to have radiation treatment five days a week in twenty-minute increments as well as take chemo pills during the entire process.

I started the procedure during the first week of March. At the end of the week I started to feel the effects. I struggled to sleep at night. The radiation burned my insides and ate away at my pelvis area I steeled myself to endure another week of torture. The chemo pills also took their toll on me. I felt tired. I lost my appetite and felt sick all the time. I couldn't walk a few yards without losing my breath. I had to walk slow and would have to find the nearest seat. For the first time in my life, I felt like an old man.

Finally, the twenty-eight days came to an end. The radiation sessions were done, and I stopped taking the pills. My nausea remained. I constantly ran to the bathroom. Sometimes I went at least eight or nine times a day. My stomach could not hold anything down.

I was hoping that the radiation would destroy the tumor so I wouldn't have to do the operation. The tumor shrunk, but it did not disappear. I needed surgery. When my doctor explained the process, I didn't like it. I did not like his attitude either. He wanted to cut my stomach down the middle from my pelvis to reach the tumor and remove it. *It sounded like he wanted to butcher me.* I needed a second opinion and fast.

Thank god for my daughter Shayla. She found another doctor who specialized in laparoscopic surgery which meant that I could have less evasive surgery with quicker recovery time. The process involved using an internal camera with two small incisions to pull out the tumor.

I scheduled the surgery for the first week of June which gave me a couple of months to recuperate from my rigorous radiation and chemo treatments. This alternative sounded a lot better. I was with it.

On surgery day, I checked into Cleveland Clinic in Weston, Florida. Besides the doctor handling the operation, he was assisted by another medical surgeon. After eight hours of surgery, I woke up high as a kite thanks to heavy medication that numbed the pain. For someone who had just had a serious operation, I was in great spirits. I cracked jokes with my family members. I was scheduled to stay in the hospital for at least three more days. Because I could not take the abdominal gas pains, I stayed for ten days.

I walked around the hallways to gain my strength back and to start my system moving again. Back in my old hip-hop days I played the wall to look cool. Now I needed it to keep my balance. I had come full circle though. The tumor was removed but I had to heal.

During the entire ordeal, I was amazed at how the human body worked. A colon has no nerve endings. Food is digested into fluid from the upper intestine. Once it hits the lower intestine it turns to solid waste. Because of the condition I had to wear an ileostomy bag attached to the right side of my stomach where my upper intestine was located. I emptied out the bag of fluid two to three times a day.

    I was also prescribed Oxycodone. It gave me some relief, but it was like trying to use a band-aid to cover a gunshot wound. Once I finished my prescription, I would still have to deal with the pain. When my supply ran out, the pain was crippling. My nerves felt like they were on fire and it felt like I was being stabbed over and over. I called my doctor for help. My pain was unbearable. I needed another prescription.

    I surfed the internet for solutions. I read how people were getting hooked on Oxycodone and couldn't get off. Oxycodone was an opioid and the addiction rate was high. I decided to stop taking it and went cold turkey on my own. It wasn't easy.

For five days, I laid in bed paralyzed with pain. I was too scared to move. I was mentally worn down from trying to block out the pain that never went away.

    My body was twisted in different directions and I resisted the urge to adjust myself because I knew I was gonna pay for it. I was weak. My body was drenched from all the cold sweats. It felt like I was being tortured. Each day never seemed to end. Twenty-four hours felt like an eternity. Now I knew what addicts went through when they went cold turkey. After five days, I turned the corner and things began to let up. I started to feel better and realized that I did not need the pills anymore.

A month later, I started my chemotherapy sessions. A small port was inserted into my upper right chest. I saw an oncologist every two weeks. I had to sit in a stationary position for at least three hours to receive chemo. When I left for the day, there was a small box machine with a tube attached to the port of my chest. It released chemo every minute as it passed through the tube.

The process was rigorous. I kept the machine with me for 48 hours and returned it to the clinic for removal every other Friday. On Monday, I came back for a booster shot to increase my immune system function. The shot wiped me out. Sometimes it was worse than the chemo. My energy levels were up and down during the week I would feel wiped out and at the end of two weeks I would gain my energy back, only to have to start my routine all over again.

I felt horrible inside. I also started to change physically. I got a yeast infection in my mouth. My tongue was the color of white chalk. The nerves in my hands and feet were gone. My hands started to peel. I couldn't touch anything cold, so I slept with socks on my feet. My taste buds disappeared. Every time the machine was attached to my chest, I had hiccups for days. When I tried to walk, my feet were tender, and my joints ached.

The chemotherapy destroyed every cell in my body. At the same time, it was constructing new ones. The push-and-pull of my recovery was excruciating.

My body felt brittle. My eyebrows were thinning out and my eyelashes disappeared. My voice sounded weak and frail. It cracked when I spoke and I barely spoke above a whisper. I sounded like the actor Clint Eastwood from those old spaghetti western flicks.

When the middle of October rolled around, I was finally finished with chemo. I was totally wiped out. I could barely do a half a pushup. By the first week of December I had the ileostomy bag removed. I ended up staying longer in the hospital for another ten days due to reoccurring gas pains. I learned that the propofol anesthesia shuts down your system and once you wake up from sedation, you need to keep moving. There is no time for sitting around or intaking food too quickly. I found that out the hard way.

I was prescribed Lyrica for my hands and feet. After six months, the nerves in my fingers came back. The pain left my hands and feet. I didn't need to take the medication anymore. I was elated. I was on my way back!

Where I'm From: Growing Up Hip Hop

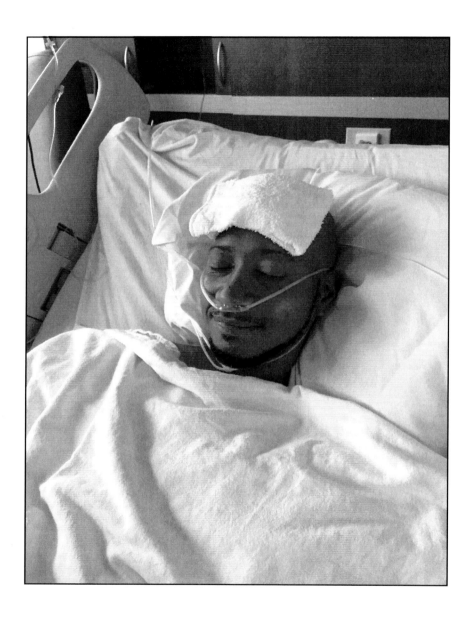

Where I'm From: Growing Up Hip Hop

Outro
Can't Stop Won't Stop

These days my feet are still numb, but most times I don't even realize or notice it. During my health challenges, I realized that we all go through something. It is about dealing with our issues the best we can.

Many of my hip-hop comrades have dealt with similar conditions or worse. Some have faced challenges without the resources or support from loved ones.

To my hip hop colleagues who have passed on, I salute your accomplishments and will always celebrate your legacies. For the others who are still here and trying to maintain in the face of adversity, I salute you too.

I am grateful for the love and support of my family and friends who continue to hold me down on my journey through life. At this point I don't sweat the small things. No arguments, fights, grudges, hatred or greed. I enjoy every day as it comes and I use my time wisely.. I fought the biggest battle of my life and I am still standing, ready to go another round. I am on my feet, still grinding as usual. Most of all, I am still staying afloat. **Thank you for reading.**

Where I'm From: Growing Up Hip Hop

DIVINES
Cleve-o (The Super 7 MCs)

One of my best friends at the time was Bernard Doss. He was a dope DJ. We called him Kid Flash, but he went by "Original B." He convinced me to get down with him to start a rap group. We called it The Super 7. They would spin off into two groups: The Turnout Brothers and the Super Lovers.

The Turnout Brothers started out with Original B--- he was the visionary. There was Markie Brown Quicksilver and me. Later, Ron and his man Wiz joined the group as the Super 7 evolved into the Super Lovers. I knew Ron from the neighborhood and spending way too much time at 127. I also knew his older sister from summer camp.

The idea of forming the Turnout Brothers was Original B's. Due to creative differences amongst the Super 7, individuals floated in and out. Others went their separate ways. Original B, Markie Brown, Quick Silver and I formed the first version of the group. Shortly after that, Kid replaced Markie Brown, Quick went Herbie, Play and Romeo to the Super Lovers. Later, Wiz came on board to the T-Bros along with Ron.

The Super Lovers were Herby, Play and Romeo---Original B's brother. The group members would evolve again when Quick left us for the Super Lovers and Kid replaced Markie. Our groups were set. As the Turnout Brothers, we made a name for ourselves by doing house parties, block parties and park jams. We made the rounds in all the MC competitions and conventions. We also performed with King Charles, Disco Twins and even with DJ Kool Herc from the Bronx. Eventually, the word got around that we were some of the "dopest" on the mic and we had an impressive DJ. The Supreme Team took notice and extended an invite to form an alliance with them and the Force MCs from Staten Island. This led to bigger and better shows and some radio play and live radio performances on the Supreme Team Show. The Turnout Brothers were a talented bunch of brothers who loved to have fun and rock a party. It was always a good time. We were always joking around, having fun and enjoying each other's company and making the best out of life.

DIVINES

Salt

The first thing that comes to mind thinking about East Elmhurst around the time the group was formed was that I was Hurby Luv Bug's girlfriend. He introduced me to East Elmhurst. What I remember most is recording in his attic. That is where I found my voice. That's where Salt N Pepa was born. Hurby's house was like Hitsville for Motown, it was where we all gathered to practice dance steps. Eventually, we started recording in Hurby's garage.

My first musical experience was on the mic, trying to figure out who I wanted to be and what I wanted to say. One thing that sticks out was performing at the Fever night club, it was like the Hip-Hop Apollo. If you could get them to like you then you were legit and Salt n Pepa killed it!!!

We recorded the Tramp video in the Latin Quarter. It was the place to be. It was hip-hop. My sister Kimberly was a dancer with B.A.D. and she introduced the dancers in the video---IOU. They already had a reputation. We rehearsed there a couple of days with them then shot the video, it was thrilling because it was our first video and we were over the moon with excitement.

Where I'm From: Growing Up Hip Hop

I don't remember when I met Ron, but I do not remember him *not* being around, Ron was a quiet genius always producing and doing his thing gleaming and perfecting his talent.

DIVINES
Hurby Luv Bug

The first thing that comes to mind when talking about East Elmhurst was the music. The second was the young ladies. Growing up there was amazing. History was made there. My first professional job was going to a session with John "Jellybean" Benitez while he was doing a remix of the Mexican at Blank Tape studios in New York. I was amazed and decided from right there this is what I wanted to do.

The first record I produced was called "The Lovers Law" by Quicksilver and the Super Lovers. I do not remember exactly when I met Ron. It seems like I always knew him. Ron was known as the guy with all the fly sisters. My favorite emcee moment I remember was when we battled The Turnout Brothers at Flushing High School and we won. I also remember when they came back for a rematch at Holliday Inn and they crushed us.

I met Salt and Pepa at the Sears Service Center in Queens where we all worked. It was very helpful for Red Alert to break anybody's record. Especially at the LQ. That was the place to be. The LQ was the only club in Manhattan that had a hip-hop night. Everybody who's anybody knew about it. My finest memory of the LQ was when they played, *I'll Take Your Man*. The crowd went crazy. Networking was always important inside the LQ. A lot of people in the business were there. We filmed Tramp--- my first video there. I will never forget it. I remember going on the road. Our Howard University show is where I first met Diddy and Derrick D-Dot. That was the first show we did for college students.

Where I'm From: Growing Up Hip Hop

DIVINES

Tone Fresh (Two Kings in A Cipher DJ)

Probably the first thing that comes to mind for me about 2 Kings in A Cipher was that we could not put the second album out. A lot of people slept on us with the first album, but real Hip Hop heads respected it. We were determined to make a solid second album and wanted to be on the same level as our peers like Tribe Called Quest, Leaders of the New School, Brand Nubian, X Clan, and Poor Righteous Teachers. We had to be on the same level as them or else we would be considered wack.

We put in some hard work and everybody stepped up. I was a lot more involved on the second album. Now I was rapping, writing, DJing and learning production, so I was amped. We had heavyweight producers lined up for the second album. Marley Marl, Grand Puba, Busta Rhymes, Skeff Anslem, a new young cat named Chucky Thompson and of course Ron. We put together a hot album and I was all over it. I was ready to show the game what I could do and unfortunately it never came out. It still bothers me till this day, but it happened for a reason. I was not mature enough to handle real success at that time because we would have become rap stars if that album came out. It was dope.

Where I'm From: Growing Up Hip Hop

It was great times back then. Living in Washington DC and being around Howard campus was pretty dope. Howard had thousands of students so meeting so many people from all over the country was cool. Mostly, all the cool New Yorkers cliqued up and hung together. We were popular, so we were VIP everywhere we went so we pretty much ran things. Because we had a record deal, an album and a few videos out which was big in the early 90's we got a lot of attention.

I loved learning about other people's hoods and cultures and would always go visit my boys and a few chicks' hoods back in Brooklyn, Bronx, Jersey, and Virginia. It was always exciting and different for me because I love to see how and where other people grew up at. Most of the New York clique did not hang with D.C. dudes but I did. My best friend E. Boogie was from New Orleans but lived in D.C., he showed me all over the DMV and we had a ball. I learned a lot about D.C. culture and met a lot of good people through him. I met a lot of lifetime friends at Howard University and it was a great experience.

The first time I met Ron was in his dorm room. My cousin Rich was a student at Howard, and he had been telling me about life at Howard University for a few years. I was in the army at the time and would visit Howard on my leave. I knew years before I got out of the army, I was going to Howard University, no question. A few months after I got out of the army, Rich calls and says "These 2 guys just got a record deal on campus and need a DJ. I told them you were the illest, but they don't believe me. You gotta get down here quick". Rich knew how good I was and did not want me to miss this opportunity. Rich kept bothering Ron about me and Ron finally said tell him to come down to audition. Rich called and I packed up the whip with my turntables, mixer and records and headed to DC. When I arrived, I hooked my turntables up in Ron's room. His roommate happened to be my man Gary from my home town. Long story short, I killed the audition right there and Ron offered me the job on the spot. He told me that we would start recording the album within a couple months and I needed to move down to DC, asap. In my head though, "I wondered what about my job? how am I gonna pay my car note? What are my parents gonna say? My answer? ---I guess I am going to Howard University!

My experience with TKO was that it was my introduction to the music business. I had some good times and some bad. I learned about the music business and found out what it was all about. I learned the recording process and how to work in the studio. I became a music producer, a good writer and produced a few songs for some major artists because of it. I learned to not confuse friendship when it comes to business and money. Always keep it business regardless who it is. I met a lot of cool people, worked with a lot of dope artists and met some musical legends. I still wish that second album would have come out!

Where I'm From: Growing Up Hip Hop

DIVINES

D- Dot

Ron's story and mine is a little more complicated because my goal was never to be a producer. I was a rapper at heart. Ron was a rapper who turned into an ill producer. Then it got to the point where we were separated. He went to LA to make some money while I was in NYC. So I said, "well Ron while I'm here let me shop some of your tracks and get some money." He was a master at this. While I'm in NY trying to hustle and get my shit off, I am also shopping Ron's track and we were selling them. So now I'm using the money to buy a drum machine and set up my home studio. I am doing beats in my own basement and then I would send them to Ron in LA. He would send me DATs and DATs of music. At the same time, I am working for Puff and also a tour manager for Mary J. Blige. So, one day I'm sitting in the room playing joints for Puff and he was like "oh my god what's that? oh my god what's that?" That's how we sold a song to Puff for a remix.

That is how the whole thing came about. For me being a producer, it was like happenstance. I was trying to go on a rap route more than a producer route. It was necessity that made it so that I became a producer. It was out of necessity. I needed to rap over shit, and I needed to make money and he was making phenomenal shit. He was making R&B joints, pop joints, Hip Hop Joints, sample joints and original joints. Ron was in LA working with Shai and the producers from there and he was developing a whole new sound. So, when he sent his music back to NYC, we got all the attention. So, I sneak my little one or two loops in there.

When he moved back to NYC that was it. I had concept because I was already a rapper. I was already laying down choruses for you, you had only to rap on it. They had no work to do, just write their rhymes and I would grab my records and go to his crib to make beats. Hand him the records, tell him the parts I wanted. He would do his thing. I was the only producer inside Bad Boy giving complete tracks to artists. I gave Tracy Lee a song with the hook on it, we gave a beat with a hook on it to The Lox before they even rapped on it. That was when I met Pharrell. He kind of inspired me because he walked in with a DAT full of songs with hooks. Pharrell was on Mase's first album and a lot of people do not know that was the Neptunes. He helped us skip the line back then in 1994-95. Nobody was really doing that. We were a unique kind of duo. We were like a full-service station, we had whatever you needed. I would sit with Ron and watch him make beats. I wanted to make beats just enough for me to rhyme over and Ron would finish them. He would rely on me telling him what people liked and he would create it. I would come down with a simple idea and Ron would create a song for me to rhyme over. That was where our producer camaraderie started. Then I would write 'cause I am a writer. I would lay hooks over his shit. The opportunity to get down with Bad Boy overextended my expectations. Me and Ron had our fifteen minutes with Two Kings in A Cipher. For us, it was like let us try it. I did not sign my contract until we came back from Trinidad. I wanted to see it to believe it. Everyone was already signed.

Where I'm From: Growing Up Hip Hop

DIVINES

Puffy

I met Ron Lawrence back when I was going to Howard in '87. I was trying to get into the music industry. I remember, there was a couple of cats in D.C. making beats and a couple of cats that went to Howard, they were making beats and rhyming and stuff like that. So, I was going around offering everybody, saying, "I can be your manager, give me a chance, let me be your manager". Everybody was looking at me like I was crazy 'cause I had no experience. I am at Howard just like they are. At the time there was nobody young in the music industry, so he said I could not be his manager. He said son, go out there and get some other clients, make some noise in the music industry and then come and hit me. So, I immediately left Howard, went and made a whole bunch of mother fucking noise, and that is why we are here right now making a whole lot of mother fucking money.

DIVINES

Younglord (Bad Boy Hitman)

I was in LA the night that Big died. That night we were at the Vibe party at the museum. I saw Big, he was in a wheelchair. Everyone was excited because the album was about to drop. At the time, I had just had my business cards. I was just a young guy passing out my cards. I ran out of cards. So, me and my cousin went to Kinkos to get some more made up, so we did not follow them. So, we are driving back on our way to a Trackmasters party and I see Big trucks. I pull over and I see Puff's security. I ask if we were still going to the party and he said "naaah, Big got shot!" I just remember looking around seeing people crying. This just happened thirty minutes ago. People were already at the hospital. I remember calling my mom before the news hit. She asked me "do you really think you should be working with these guys?" It was a very sad time. He had a lot more music in 'em . We lost a legend.

Where I'm From: Growing Up Hip Hop

DIVINES

Brooke Richardson (songwriter)

There were several hands that led me to the legendary Ron "Amen-Ra" Lawrence and I am grateful for each hand because to this day I know, respect, and consider Ron my friend. I am a native Memphian and in 2002, I was working with Isaac Hayes in a (song) writing capacity. He was based in NYC and the acting assistant to his company was Michelle Spence. She was acquainted with Haqq Islam, CEO of University Records and Haqq arranged our introduction. I was able to meet with him and get CD's with his tracks so that I could work on lyrics and melodies.

When I found out Luther was considering the song Ron and I wrote together, I was thrilled. The song Luther Vandross chose was originally penned for a female singer. Ron told me to modify it for a male vocalist and he later asked me to add a bridge. I was excited about the prospect, but I remember the experience feeling very surreal. It was always a very natural creative process with Ron. His home studio was very cozy and comfortable; he would play tracks and allow me to choose which I would write. In many cases Ron had a clear direction of what he wanted as it related to style and subject matter.

Where I'm From: Growing Up Hip Hop

It was easy to follow his direction. Other times, he would just let me go. He did not micromanage; he would leave me and go upstairs and check back to listen when I finished. Working in the studio with Ron did not feel like work; however, I learned so much. He was one of the first established producers that I had worked and recorded with.

When I heard the finished recording of the record Ron and I wrote for Luther Vandross, I was outdone. I remember going to the record store, looking for it, finding it, seeing our song listed on the song list and feeling overwhelmed and blessed.

DIVINES

Tyrese

Ron Lawrence and I met at the Best Western Presidential Hotel through my management, Greg Parks. First Ron just came over to see Greg 'cause they knew each other, and he ended up coming up to RCA to play some tracks. Ron Lawrence…quiet, humble, focused and simple. Yeah, cool peoples. Dealing with somebody like Ron I can tell that he does not like taking no BS in the studio. And all this traffic and stuff, it ain't really his forte and that causes me to tell my peoples to get out and let's get jstuff done. He is talented. Now, this is my first album and I can only see him getting better and working with better people and making history, futuristically speaking. I see myself working with him again, of course.

DIVINES

Benny Medina Interlude (music exec)

It is like working with a real professional, working with a real artist, working with somebody who cares about artists and cares about the music. When you think about what he has done with Biggie, with Faith, with The Lox, with Mase and with Puff, it really all speaks for itself. You know, he is sort of the quite energy around the Hitmen who continuously delivers. It seems to me like that even most recently, the Faith record was in one place and then *"Love Like This"* came along and just jump started it. Like back in the day, Berry Gordy always had his ringers. When the record was just about finished, he would go to Norman Whitfield, when the record was just about finished, he would go to, Smokey Robinson. When the record is just about finished, Puffy usually goes…to Lawrence!

Where I'm From: Growing Up Hip Hop